The
Gardener's
Yearbook

About the Author

Martyn Cox is gardening columnist with the *Mail on Sunday*, the UK's most read Sunday paper, a post he has held for more than 15 years. He writes regularly for many other titles, both print and online. He is a guest presenter on gardening shows at shopping TV channel TJC and is the author of 11 books, including the bestselling *The Veg Grower's Almanac* (BBC Books).

Martyn is a qualified horticulturist and has many years' practical gardening experience. Prior to becoming a freelance writer, he was on the staff at *Gardenlife, BBC Gardeners' World* magazine, *Amateur Gardening* and *Horticulture Week*. He shares a small garden on the south coast with his family and two dogs.

Martyn Cox

The Gardener's Yearbook

A month-by-month guide
to getting the most from your plot

ILLUSTRATIONS BY HEATHER TEMPEST-ELLIOTT

MITCHELL BEAZLEY

First published in Great Britain in 2022 by Mitchell Beazley, an imprint of
Octopus Publishing Group Ltd
Carmelite House
50 Victoria Embankment
London EC4Y 0DZ
www.octopusbooks.co.uk

An Hachette UK Company
www.hachette.co.uk

Distributed in the US by
Hachette Book Group
1290 Avenue of the Americas
4th and 5th Floors
New York, NY 10104

Distributed in Canada by
Canadian Manda Group
664 Annette St.
Toronto, Ontario, Canada M6S 2C8

ISBN 978-1-78472-815-1

A CIP catalogue record for this book is available from the British Library.

Printed and bound in Europe

10 9 8 7 6 5 4 3 2 1

Publisher: Alison Starling
Editor: Sarah Kyle
Art Director & Designer: Yasia Williams
Illustrator: Heather Tempest-Elliott
Assistant Production Managers: Lucy Carter and Nic Jones

Contents

Introduction

I want to start by telling you a story. In the early 1970s, my parents bought a house together and were faced with looking after a garden for the first time. It might have been on the small side but it was a daunting prospect for the young, recently married couple as neither had any gardening experience. Both had grown up in families whose outdoor space consisted of a concrete backyard containing an outdoor loo, coal shed and little else. Because of their unfamiliarity with gardens, they had no idea when to prune the shrubs they'd inherited, how to maintain their lawn or what action to take after aphids descended upon their roses. Rather than carrying on aimlessly, they bought a copy of *The Gardening Year*, a book published by Reader's Digest in 1969. Apart from providing the sage advice required to tend their garden, the book gave them the skills to plant bulbs, grow vegetables from scratch and even take on practical projects like building a rock garden. I can clearly recall my mum and dad taking the practical tome off the bookshelf and referring to its pages for advice. On a recent trip 'home', I decided to delve into its pages. Fifty years or so after publication, a lot of the information in the well-thumbed book was well past its sell-by date, in everything from gardening techniques to pest control.

Yet, despite being outdated, the concept of the book was sound, and it inspired me to write one that would help today's gardeners get to grips with their plot. You won't find mentions of noxious chemicals or tips on laying crazy paving in the title you are currently holding, but you will unearth spadefuls of down-to-earth, contemporary advice.

As our gardens are very much driven by the seasons, this book has been divided into 12 sections that will let you know what you can be doing to keep on top of the garden each month. There are also gentle reminders at certain times of the year to sow seeds, plant things, make features, harvest crops and to look out for pests and diseases.

Yet this is not just a practical gardening book. I'm a great believer that gardening should be fun, thought-provoking and entertaining. For that reason, I've peppered the pages with interesting facts, trivia and gardening lore. So, even when you're not gardening, there will be some nuggets of information waiting for you to find inside.

For me, one of the great joys of gardening is seeing how your outdoor space changes during the seasons. In my opinion, nothing lifts the spirits more after a long winter than spotting the shoots of bulbs nosing their way above ground in spring. Elsewhere, blossom decorates branches and buds burst open as leaves start to unfurl. Summer announces its arrival with an oomph, as roses, climbers and perennials flower their socks off, and the garden is at its most voluminous. In early autumn, the vegetable garden is brimming with produce, and later in the season the foliage of many deciduous trees and shrubs turns fiery shades before falling.

Apart from keeping us in touch with the rhythm of the seasons, the changes to our gardens act as prompts that certain tasks are required - it's important to keep on top of what needs doing to prevent things getting out of hand and to fully enjoy your space. Some jobs are seasonal; others more regular. Weeding can be an all-year-round affair.

So, whether you're a complete newbie or have earned your gardening stripes, have a large garden or a really small one, want to grow your own edibles or raise ornamental plants, I hope this book provides you with the know-how to keep your garden in good shape and helps to increase your gardening knowledge to take it to the next level.

'What can be said in New Year rhymes,

That's not been said a thousand times?

The new years come, the old years go,

We know we dream, we dream we know.'

(Ella Wheeler Wilcox, *The Year*)

THE MONTH AT A GLANCE

- Remove tatty leaves from hellebores (*Helleborus*).
- Hoick out annual weeds.
- Gather birch and hazel twigs to make supports for herbaceous plants.
- Winter prune wisterias (see How to Prune Wisteria, page 136).
- Take hardwood cuttings of trees and shrubs (see Take Hardwood Cuttings, page 226).
- Take root cuttings from shrubs and perennials (see How To Take Root Cuttings, page 238).
- Plant deciduous hedges.
- Cut back stems of autumn-fruiting raspberries to ground level (see Pruning Raspberry Canes, page 228).
- Cover autumn-sown broad beans during severe cold spells.
- Check on stored edibles, throwing out any that are soft or rotting.
- Comb your hand through soft-leaved grasses, to remove debris.
- Remove large stones from the surface of autumn-sown lawns.
- Keep off the lawn in frosty weather, to avoid damaging the grass.
- Dig soil during mild spells.
- Keep bird feeders topped up.
- Remove ice from birdbaths and top up with fresh water.
- Float balls in ponds to prevent freezing.
- Clean and sharpen gardening tools.
- Place an order for seeds.
- Keep houseplants in good shape by snipping off dead flowers and tatty foliage.

January

The start of a new year is the traditional time for gardeners to take stock of their gardens, reflecting on the ups and downs of the past 12 months. But this is not just a chance to mull over days gone by. As it's generally a quiet time in the garden, and often very cold, this is a good opportunity for a spot of armchair gardening. Use the downtime to order seeds for sowing in spring and making plans that will shape your space in the months ahead. Of course, if you are itching to get outdoors, there are still things to be done.

↓ Prevent the spread of hellebore leaf spot disease by pruning infected plants. Completely remove and destroy tainted foliage, leaving only flowering stems.

Trim Hellebores

Hellebores (*Helleborus*) provide a much-needed splash of colour early in the year but these plants are vulnerable to a fungal disease known as hellebore leaf spot. Leaves of infected plants are dotted with unsightly brown or black patches that eventually fall out to leave a ragged appearance, while flower buds can rot and shoots collapse. Prevent the spread of this disease by immediately cutting off any blighted leaves, putting them on a bonfire or in the dustbin to ensure the fungal spores are destroyed. Some gardeners like to go one step further and completely defoliate plants in early winter, leaving just the flower stems behind (see opposite). Fresh leaves will appear in spring.

Tackle Weeds

Annual weeds are opportunistic little blighters that will quickly colonize bare soil when your back is turned. A cold snap helps to curb their germination and will even kill some weeds, but if the weather is mild, then they will pop up like crazy wherever there's a gap, from beds to the tops of pots. It's easy to turn a blind eye to them when they are small, but if you ignore weeds the problem will soon get out of hand. Rather than spending hours trying to get on top of an infestation, carry out a five-minute blitz once a week - you won't get them all but it will help keep them under control. Most annual weeds are easy enough to tug up by hand, while a hoe is best for covering larger areas.

FIVE ANNOYING ANNUALS

1 **Annual nettle** (*Urtica urens*) -
sometimes called small stinging nettle;
this forms a bushy plant up to 50cm
(20in) tall and has an average of
1,000 seeds per plant. Remember to
wear gloves when handling, to avoid
being stung.

2 **Chickweed** (*Stellaria media*) - a
vigorous spreading plant forming
a mat of small, bright green, oval
leaves and tiny white flowers. An
individual plant can give rise to 1,300
seeds. Its appearance is an indicator of
good soil fertility.

3 **Groundsel** (*Senecio vulgaris*) - a
bushy plant up to 60cm (24in) in
height, with long lobed leaves and
small yellow flowers. It acts as a host
to cineraria rust disease, which can
spread to ornamental plants.

4 **Hairy bittercress** (*Cardamine hirsuta*)
- each seed pod on this rosette-forming
plant is packed with about 20 seeds,
which are fired up to 1m (3ft) in the air
when you brush past them. An average
plant can carry about 600 seeds.

5 **Sun spurge** (*Euphorbia helioscopia*)
- a compact plant topped with bright
yellow flowers from mid-spring until
late summer. A single plant is capable
of producing 700 seeds that can
remain viable for 20 years.

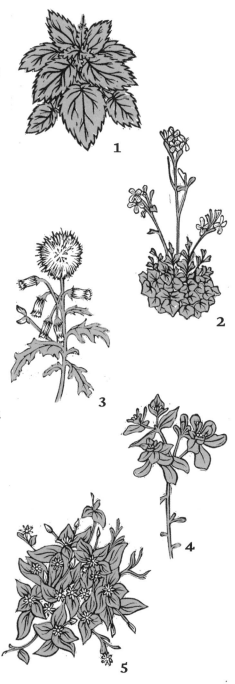

Order Seeds

When the weather is poor outside, nothing beats leafing through seed catalogues or scrolling through online lists and dreaming about what you'll be sowing in a few weeks' time. Alas, when faced with so many tempting edibles and flowers, it's easy to get carried away and order far more than you'll ever get round to sowing or actually have room for in your garden. The best approach is to make a long wish list, and then revisit it a day or two later, ruthlessly editing it down to something more realistic.

Feed Birds

Birds have a tough time over winter, especially during a prolonged cold snap or snowy weather. Do your bit to help them through tough times by ensuring they always have fresh water and by installing some feeders filled with high-energy food. Birds then stand a much better chance of making it through the next few months.

CHOOSING FEEDING DEVICES

A hanging bird table will be popular among shy species, although some birds prefer to dine from a ground feeding table. Suspend tubular feeders from the branches of a tree or mount them on a feeder pole set in a lawn or border If squirrels are a problem, choose a feeder protected by a wire cage or baffle.

PICKING BIRD FOOD

There are numerous different seed mixes for feeders, some containing exotic fare like dried insects, raisins, oyster-shell grit, mung beans and suet pellets. But you don't really need anything fancy. Kibbled peanuts or shelled sunflower hearts are ideal as they are oil- and fat-rich, providing birds with plenty of energy.

Word buster:
Fasciation

A genetic mutation of the growing tip of some plants that results in the production of flattened, elongated shoots and flowerheads. Despite being unsightly, fasciation is completely harmless and does not affect the vigour of plants. Forsythias, daphnes and delphiniums are all prone to this phenomenon.

WHERE TO PUT FEEDERS

Birds will only use feeders if they feel safe from predators, so put them in a spot where the birds have a clear view of the garden and can fly to cover if frightened. Ideally, place a feeder no more than 2.1m (7ft) away from a tree, shrub or hedge. Avoid putting feeders above dense shrubs, where cats can hide and mount surprise attacks.

DON'T FORGET THE WATER

Birds also need plenty of water for drinking and bathing. Keep birdbaths, dishes and hanging bowls topped up and knock out any ice that develops during a cold snap. Floating a table-tennis ball or twig on the surface helps as it will move about and prevent ice from forming.

Propagate Supermarket Herbs

Pick a well-filled pot of coriander (*Coriandrum sativum*), chives (*Allium schoenoprasum*), mint (*Mentha*), parsley (*Petroselinum*), basil (*Ocimum*) or similar clump-forming herb, then carefully divide the rootball into four smaller portions and replant each into a small pot. Water well and place in a light spot indoors. Don't worry if the stems wilt to begin with - this is perfectly normal and the plant will soon perk up. Avoid picking any of the leaves until the plant shows signs of actively growing. Move the herbs into slightly larger pots when necessary and outdoors in the summer months.

Nature's Air Fresheners

Let's face it, very few gardens smell good in winter. Damp air, soggy soil and decaying plant matter combine to make an unsavoury cocktail. Fortunately, there are loads of shrubs with scented flowers that will freshen the air and give you a good reason to go outside when the weather is cold.

FIVE GREAT FRAGRANT WINNERS

1 **Christmas box** (*Sarcococca confusa*) - produces clusters of heavily scented, spidery, white flowers and glossy black berries, displayed against dark, wavy, oval leaves.

2 **Gold-edged winter daphne** (*Daphne odora* 'Aureomarginata') - a compact variegated shrub with shoots that are topped with clusters of perfumed, pale pink flowers in January and February.

3 *Hamamelis* × *intermedia* **'Orange Peel'** - the bare branches of this witch hazel are adorned with light orange flowers with a scent similar Seville orange marmalade.

4 *Mahonia* × *media* **'Charity'** - sprays of sweetly scented, yellow flowers top tall stems clothed with glossy, prickly leaves from November to March.

5 **Wintersweet** (*Chimonanthus praecox*) - the bare branches of wintersweet bear masses of heavily scented, pendulous, pale yellow flowers from November to March.

APPLE WASSAILING

Apple wassailing is a curious custom that is believed to have started in the orchards of southwest England. Taking place on Twelfth Night (7 January), groups of men and boys would parade from orchard to orchard, where they would carry out a ritual aimed at encouraging trees to produce a good crop in autumn. They would hit trees with sticks to wake them up from winter dormancy and blow cow horns to scare evil spirits away, while chanting rhymes and guzzling cider. The word wassailing comes from the Saxon *waes hael*, meaning 'be well', and the tradition has been carried on for centuries, with its roots going back to pre-Christian times.

'Stand fast root, bear well top.

Pray the God send us a howling good crop.

Every twig, apples big.

Every bough, apples now.'

19th-century wassailing rhyme

Create Hedges

A hedge makes a cracking physical boundary, but they are not just for defining our plots or hiding us from nosy neighbours. These essential garden features have a multitude of uses, from providing security to reducing noise from busy roads, and from acting as a windbreak to giving gardens their structure. Of course, hedges also possess the kind of looks that makes them an attractive addition in their own right.

FORMAL AND INFORMAL

Hedges basically fall into two camps based on their shape: formal and informal. Formal hedges are clipped tightly to provide a geometric look that suits a variety of garden styles, from contemporary to classic. They require regular cutting over summer. Informal hedges are not clipped hard, and they are left to produce flowers, fruit and berries. They suit a more relaxed style, such as a wildlife garden or traditional cottage garden. Informal hedges take up more space than formal ones.

FIVE GREAT PLANTS FOR AN INFORMAL HEDGE

1   golden barberry (*Berberis × stenophylla*)

2   *Escallonia rubra* var. *macrantha*

3   *Forsythia × intermedia* 'Lynwood Gold'

4   snowberry (*Symphoricarpos albus* var. *laevigatus*)

5   *Weigela* 'Florida Variegata'

FIVE GREAT PLANTS FOR A FORMAL HEDGE

1   cherry laurel (*Prunus laurocerasus*)

2   copper beech (*Fagus sylvatica* Atropurpurea Group)

3   Lawson's cypress (*Chamaecyparis lawsoniana*)

4   Portuguese laurel (*Prunus lusitanica*)

5   common yew (*Taxus baccata*)

DID YOU KNOW ?

Towering above a stretch of the A93 in Highland Perthshire is the largest hedge on the planet - a 20m (60ft)-high and 0.5km (0.3-mile) long bulwark that was planted in 1745 by Jean Mercer and her husband, Robert Murray Nairne. Given its proportions, it's no surprise that the Meikleour beech hedge holds the records for tallest in the world and longest in Britain.

1   Prepare the ground well. Remove weeds and dig over the soil, working in some organic matter.

2   If you are planning on planting an internal hedge in a lawn, strip away a 90cm (36in)-wide band of grass, with a spade.

3   A single row of plants is suitable for most hedges, but a double row (two single rows in parallel) will make it more animal-proof. Allow 45cm (18in) between rows, and stagger plants along each, rather than planting them directly opposite.

4   Mark out the course of a hedge with a bricklayer's line and lay out plants, 30-60cm (12-24in) apart, depending on the variety. Make individual planting holes, or dig a straight-sided trench 60cm (24in) wide and 43cm (17in) deep.

5   Place the plants in the holes or trench, making sure bare-root ones are at the same level as they were growing previously. Replace the soil and gently firm into place with your heel.

6   Give the plants a good soaking and finish by spreading a 7.5cm (3in) layer of mulch around them to lock in moisture and to prevent weeds germinating.

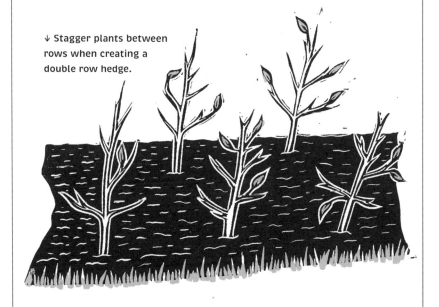

↓ Stagger plants between rows when creating a double row hedge.

BARE-ROOT OR CONTAINER-GROWN PLANTS?

You can create a hedge from bare-root or container-grown plants. Bare-root plants are much cheaper than their container-grown counterparts, making them more cost-effective when establishing a long hedge; they are available from late autumn until early spring, when bare-root plants are dormant. Deciduous hedging subjects such as beech (*Fagus*), hawthorn (*Crataegus*) and hornbeam (*Carpinus*), are commonly offered as bare roots, while evergreen ones like elaeagnus, cherry laurel (*Prunus laurocerasus*), Portuguese laurel (*P. lusitanica*) and privet (*Ligustrum*) are usually sold in containers.

WILDLIFE HEDGE

A wildlife hedge is an informal one that includes trees and shrubs with berries, flowers, fruits and nuts, which will attract beneficial creatures. It is typically composed of 60-70 per cent hawthorn (*Crataegus*) with four or five other genera. Plants to consider include field maple (*Acer campestre*), hazel (*Corylus*), spindle (*Euonymus*), blackthorn (*Prunus spinosa*) and crab apple (*Malus*). Once established, train native climbers into the hedge and underplant with wild flowers.

Trivia time

The first real gardening book to be published in England was the rather snappily titled *A most briefe and pleasaunte treatise teachyng how to dresse, sowe and set a garden*. Written by Thomas Hill and running to just 42 pages, it was published in about 1558.

DID YOU KNOW ?

Allotment plots are traditionally quoted in rods, a unit of measurement that dates back to Anglo-Saxon times and is named after a long wooden stick that was used by farmers to guide their oxen. The length of a rod varied until it was standardized in the 17th century at just over 5m (16ft). A full-size plot is usually ten square rods, roughly 250 square metres, the equivalent of a tennis court. Due to high demand, most allotment societies now provide plots that measure five square rods.

Check Your Spade

During the growing season, spades are used on a regular basis, often without getting any maintenance to keep them in good working order. Lack of upkeep will almost certainly reduce their effective life, so spend a few minutes giving yours an overhaul. If wooden handles have started to split, rub with fine sandpaper until smooth and then protect the wood by treating it with linseed or walnut oil. Spread a small amount of oil on a cloth and work it into the grain with a circular motion. Wipe down, to remove any excess oil. Over time, cutting edges can become blunt, making it hard to slice through heavy soil, so restore the edge with a flat engineer's file. Prevent a build-up of rust and stop mud sticking to the surface by wiping with oil.

Pest and Disease Watch: Scale Insects

Limpet-like scale insects are a problem on houseplants and on some outdoor plants, sucking sap and excreting a sticky substance called honeydew that provides a surface for sooty moulds to grow on. These pests are generally found on stems and underneath leaves. If spotted early enough, the odd insect can be rubbed off by hand, but larger infestations will need to be controlled with organic sprays or biological control nematodes.

→ There are many different types of sap-sucking scale insects, which can be found on a wide range of indoor and outdoor plants.

PROJECT: Make a Simple Garden Path

Paths are more than just functional devices to get us from A to B. They can be used to direct movement, lead the eye to a focal point or to delineate a space into different areas. A path allows access to the garden in poor weather and lets you get close to plants. Some require the expertise of a qualified specialist but paths with loose fillings are quick and easy to create.

YOU WILL NEED

- sand
- spade
- edging (bricks, rope-top tiles or flexible steel strips)
- landscape fabric
- tent pegs
- gravel, slate, shingle or bark
- rake

HOW TO DO IT

1 Mark out the route of the path using dry sand - paths should be at least 60cm (24in) wide for wheelbarrows.

2 Dig out the path to 5cm (2in) deep. Roughly flatten and compact it by walking over the dug area.

3 Put edging in place. Upended bricks or rope-top tiles are easily fixed on a bed of mortar.

4 Lay landscape fabric along the path recess and hold in place with tent pegs.

5 Cover the landscape fabric with a 5cm (2in) layer of your chosen material. Don't make it any deeper or you'll sink into the surface. Rake to level.

De-ice Ponds

Sub-zero temperatures lead to ponds freezing over, and if you have fish or aquatic wildlife, you'll need to take steps to allow them to breathe. One way to ensure there's an ice-free hole is to float a plastic ball on the surface. The ice will freeze around it but the space underneath will remain clear. Another way is to boil a pan of water and then place it on the ice. Depending on the thickness of the ice, you may have to repeat the process several times until a hole has melted through.

↓ Fish and amphibious wildlife are at risk if ponds freeze over in winter. Allow noxious gases to escape and oxygen to enter by keeping a patch ice-free.

'He comes, – he comes, – the frost spirit comes, you may trace his footsteps now,

On the naked woods and the blasted fields and the brown hill's withered brow.

He has smitten the leaves of the grey old trees where their pleasant green came forth,

And the winds, which follow wherever he goes, have shaken them down to earth.'

(J G Whittier, *The Frost Spirit*)

THE MONTH AT A GLANCE

- Brush off snow from plants.
- Deadhead winter bedding plants.
- Prune dogwoods (*Cornus*) and other shrubs grown for their winter stems (see Pruning for Winter Stems, page 29).
- Check tree ties and tighten any that have loosened in windy weather.
- Prune summer-flowering, deciduous shrubs (see When to Prune Shrubs, page 29).
- Plant begonia tubers indoors (see Start Begonia Tubers, page 26).
- Buy and plant snowdrops (*Galanthus*) 'in the green'.
- Plant lily bulbs in the ground or pots (see How to Grow Lilies, page 30).
- Chit seed potatoes indoors (see Time to Start Potatoes, page 34).
- Plant fig (*Ficus*) trees (see Plant a Fig Tree, page 36).
- Buy and plant shallot bulbs in the ground (see Grow Shallots, page 32).
- Plant Jerusalem artichoke tubers.
- Give summer- and autumn-flowering heathers a light trim.
- Mulch beds and borders (see Mulch Soil, page 26).
- Sweep up fallen leaves and flowers from greenhouse plants, to prevent the spread of fungal diseases.
- Cut back ornamental grasses.
- Rejuvenate soil compacted by winter wet by forking over.
- Put together a crop rotation plan (see Make a Crop Rotation Plan page 39).
- Protect early flowers on fruit trees from frost with horticultural fleece.
- Take measures to prevent slugs and snails eating emerging shoots of perennials (see Stop Slugs Eating Hostas, page 38).

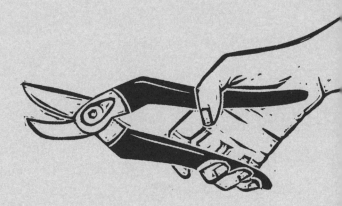

February

Snow, sleet, rain, frost and gusty blasts are all too
common in late winter, so make the most of any
dry sunny days to carry out a spot of gardening –
remember to wrap up warm as the weather can be
perishingly cold. The good news is that winter is
loosening its grip. Early flowering bulbs are starting
to add a splash of colour to the monochrome scene,
perennials are poking their noses above the ground,
and buds are starting to swell on trees and shrubs.
At last! Spring is just around the corner.

Plant Snowdrops 'In the Green'

Pot-grown snowdrops (*Galanthus*) are widely available in late winter but they can be expensive, especially if you're looking to create a bit of spectacle. If this is the case, it's far more economical to snap up bare-root plants that are still actively growing or 'in the green'. Choose a spot in dappled shade and improve the soil with leafmould or garden compost to ensure it doesn't dry out in summer. Dig a small hole with a trowel and then place a plant in the centre. Backfill with soil, ensuring each bulb is the same depth as it was before being lifted from the ground - the point where the green leaves start to turn yellow should end up level with the soil surface. Rare snowdrops often sell for a lot of money. In 2015, a single bulb of *Galanthus plicatus* 'Golden Fleece' was bought on eBay for £1,390 (plus £4 for postage and packaging), making it the most expensive snowdrop in the world.

FIVE PARTS OF LONDON NAMED AFTER PLANTS

1 Gospel Oak

2 Nine Elms

3 Poplar

4 Primrose Hill

5 Shepherd's Bush

A POTTED HISTORY OF SNOWDROPS

Common snowdrop (*Galanthus nivalis*) can be found growing wild across the UK but this ubiquitous flower is not a native to our shores. It comes from mainland Europe and is thought by some to have arrived with the Romans, although the first record of it growing wild in the countryside dates to 1778. The craze for snowdrops took off in the middle part of the 19th century. Soldiers returning from the Crimean War brought home bulbs of varieties indigenous to the Caucasus. Many more were introduced by plant hunters, and breeding work has led to a staggering number of different varieties.

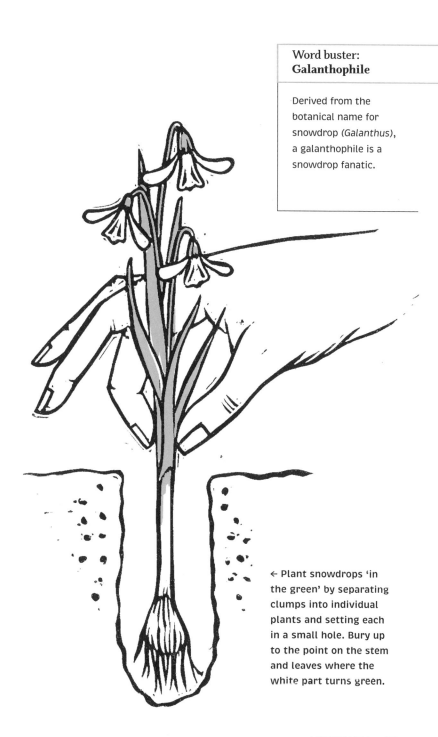

Word buster:
Galanthophile

Derived from the botanical name for snowdrop (*Galanthus*), a galanthophile is a snowdrop fanatic.

← Plant snowdrops 'in the green' by separating clumps into individual plants and setting each in a small hole. Bury up to the point on the stem and leaves where the white part turns green.

Start Begonia Tubers

Hybrid tuberous begonias (*Begonia* × *tuberhybrida*) are summer-flowering, tender perennials that are started from brown, flattened, disc-shaped tubers covered with a mass of hairy roots. Getting them going is easy.

Larger ones, 5cm (2in) or more in diameter, can be planted in containers, 10-12cm (4-5in) wide, of peat-free, multipurpose potting compost. Make sure the curved side is facing down and the hollow side up (tiny pink or white embryonic shoots might be visible). Twist the tuber into the compost until the top is just beneath the surface. Some gardeners leave tubers just proud of the surface, but this will reduce vigour as they have the ability to create roots across their entire exterior. Water and place pots inside a windowsill propagator to encourage rapid growth. In two or three weeks, sprouts should appear, and pots can be moved to a light spot out of direct sunlight. Try an east- or north-facing window ledge or set them back from a south-facing one. Water regularly to ensure healthy growth.

Start smaller tubers off in smaller pots or plant several in a seed tray - space them out evenly, making sure they are not touching to avoid rotting. Prise tubers out of the seed tray when the shoots are about 7.5cm (3in) tall and pot them up individually. Once fully grown, they can be planted directly into their final containers from the end of May onward.

Mulch Soil

Mulching is an odd-sounding term that essentially means covering the soil with a blanket of organic material such as composted bark, leafmould, well-rotted farmyard manure or garden compost. Apart from providing a dark foil that will set off shrubs, perennials and bulbs perfectly, mulch helps to provide nutrients to plants as it rots, locks in moisture and forms a barrier against weeds. The material will also insulate the roots of vulnerable plants from winter cold and protect them from extremes of heat in summer.

Before mulching, clear the site of weeds and water the soil if it is dry. Spread a 10cm (4in) layer of your chosen material across the whole area and rake to leave a level finish - wear gloves if you are handling manure or composted straw. Take care not to smother low-growing plants or to pile mulches up against the stems of woody plants. As a rule, it's best to leave a gap around stems so that the mulch does not come into contact with the bark - this can lead to the bark softening and rotting at the base and leave plants more vulnerable to diseases.

Word buster:
Mulch

It is thought that the
word mulch comes from
the Old English 'melsc',
meaning soft.

↓ Wear gloves when handling
mulches and spread them around
plants using a fork or rake.
Maintain a gap around the stems
of trees and shrubs to prevent
the material softening bark,
potentially leading to rotting.

Prune Ornamental Grasses

Deciduous ornamental grasses will soon be pumping out lots of new growth, so prune plants while they are still largely dormant. Hold clumps of pennisetum, deschampsia, hakonechloa and similar deciduous grasses in one hand and cut back with secateurs to just above ground level, avoiding any emerging growth. Follow this by spreading a 7.5cm (3in) mulch of garden compost or similar around plants. Evergreen grasses don't need such rough treatment. Put on a pair of gardening gloves and comb your hands through to remove any debris that's trapped in the clumps and also snip off any damaged growth.

FIVE GREAT GRASSES

1 *Deschampsia cespitosa* 'Goldtau' - tufted hair grass boasts tall stems carrying feathery flowers above mounds of dark green leaves. H 90cm (36in).

2 *Hakonechloa macra* SUNFLARE - a lovely Japanese forest grass that forms a clump of vibrant yellow leaves with crimson highlights. H 45cm (18in).

3 *Miscanthus sinensis* 'Ferner Osten' - feathery red flowers are carried above robust clumps of green leaves that turn copper in autumn. H 2.1m (7ft).

4 *Molinia caerulea* subsp. *caerulea* 'Variegata' - a showy grass producing feathery flowers above tufts of cream and green leaves. H 1.2m (4ft).

5 *Panicum virgatum* 'Heavy Metal' - bolt upright clumps of metallic-blue foliage are topped by a haze of purplish flowers in autumn. H 1.2-1.5m (4-5ft).

WHAT PRUNING TOOLS DO I NEED ?

Before pruning anything in the garden, make sure you've got the right tools for the job. A pair of secateurs are great for cutting shoots up to pencil thickness, while loppers are useful for shoots that are slightly thicker or harder to reach. If you have lots of tall trees or shrubs in your garden, it may also be worth buying a pair of telescopic, long-reach pruners. A handheld pruning saw or traditional bow saw will make light work of much chunkier branches.

'A weed is just a flower growing in the wrong place.'

George Washington Carver

When to Prune Shrubs

Deciduous shrubs flowering from mid-summer onward produce blooms on new shoots borne in spring and are best pruned in late winter. Those that flower in spring and early summer tend to bloom on wood generated the previous year; prune these soon after flowering, to avoid removing sleeping buds. Wait until April or May to tackle evergreen shrubs. This will ensure that any sappy tender growth stimulated by pruning is not damaged by late frosts.

PRUNING FOR WINTER STEMS

Dogwoods (*Cornus*), willows (*Salix*) and ornamental brambles (*Rubus*) are prized for their vibrant naked winter stems. In the past, gardeners were advised to cut these shrubs back hard in early spring, to leave a low stubby framework - a flush of fresh stems would then appear from the base. However, it's thought this method weakens plants over time, so simply remove one-third of the older stems. You will still get plenty of zingy young shoots but will have a larger plant that will make more impact.

» GENERAL RULES OF SHRUB PRUNING «

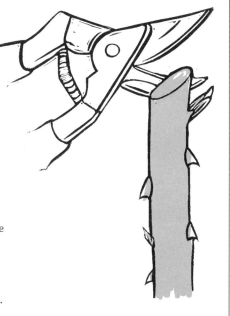

- ° Aim to end up with a shrub that possesses an open, vase-like shape, slenderer at the bottom than at the top.

- ° Start by removing the three Ds: dead, diseased or damaged growth. This will improve the looks of the shrub and will prevent infection spreading to healthy parts of the plant.

- ° Snip off thin wispy shoots, trim back wayward branches and cut out any crossing shoots. Then take out a few of the older stems from the centre to improve air and light flow.

- ° Always prune to an outward-facing bud. Use a 45-degree cut, slanted away from the bud.

How to Grow Lilies

Lilies (*Lilium*) are a versatile tribe that can be grown in beds, borders and containers, and boast flowers in a range of shapes, colours and sizes - many infused with a potent perfume. Easy to look after, lilies will come back year after year with very little fuss. Young plants in pots are readily available in mid- to late spring but you'll have a bigger choice by starting plants from bulbs.

WHERE TO GROW

Lilies are happy in sun or partial shade, and are not particularly fussy about soil as long as it's fairly fertile and free-draining. Taller varieties are ideal set against walls or fences, or planted at the back of borders, while shorter forms can be used to punctuate beds and borders. Taller forms, in particular, prefer a sheltered spot.

PLANTING BULBS IN THE GROUND

Set bulbs in holes three times their length - if you have clay soil, sprinkle some horticultural grit in the bottom to improve drainage and prevent the bulbs from rotting. For maximum impact, plant bulbs in groups of three to five, giving them plenty of room to grow by spacing them 20cm (8in) apart.

GROWING IN POTS

Lilies look particularly good in long-Tom terra-cotta pots, which have a tall, narrow shape that accentuates the form of the flower, and are heavy enough to avoid being blown over by wind. Cover drainage holes with bits of broken pot to prevent them from getting clogged up, and then half fill with compost - use John Innes No 2 or a specialist bulb planting compost. Arrange three to five bulbs on top before covering with compost, so the bulbs are 10cm (4in) below the surface. Water well.

A POTTED HISTORY OF LILIES

Native to Europe, Asia and North America, lilies are bulbous perennials that go by the botanical name of *Lilium*. They are divided into eight different groups based on their blooms. Among these are the trumpet hybrids and martagon hybrids, otherwise known as Turk's caps because of their swept-back petals.

A WORD OF WARNING:

According to the Royal Society for the Prevention of Cruelty to Animals, all parts of the lily plant are toxic to cats, including the leaves and petals. Brushing past flowers can result in pollen attaching to their coats, which might be ingested while grooming. If you're at all worried, don't bother growing any lilies.

SUPPORTING PLANTS

Compact lilies don't need staking, but those with taller or multiheaded stems are at risk from snapping under their own weight. Shore up with canes inserted next to plants, ensuring there's enough length to support two-thirds of the stem. Fasten together with soft twine tied in a figure-of-eight form.

Growing Tips

Water lilies regularly during the growing season and remove fading flowers to prevent the formation of seedheads. Cut the main stem to ground level when it turns brown in autumn, then cover with a 7.5cm (3in) mulch of garden compost or leafmould to insulate from frost, and move pots into a greenhouse, shed or front porch.

FIVE GREAT LILIES FOR SCENT

1 **'Casa Blanca'** - pure white, sweetly scented blooms, measuring 20cm (8in) across, are held on 1.2m (4ft) stems during June and July.

2 **dwarf Formosa lily** *(L. formosanum* var. *pricei)* - a knee-high beauty with flowers that match those of a regal lily for size and perfume.

3 **'Muscadet'** - beautifully perfumed sprays of white flowers, adorned with maroon spots, are carried on 90cm (36in) stems in July.

4 **regal lily** *(L. regale)* - a vintage favourite with pink buds held on 1.2m (4ft) stems that open into huge white trumpets that ooze a knockout scent.

5 **'Star Gazer'** - introduced in the 1970s, this Oriental type delivers a rich exotic scent from its pink flowers with darker spots and white edges.

WHAT ARE TREE LILIES?

Looking like lilies on steroids, tree lilies produce towering stems that are capable of carrying up to 30 dinner-plate-sized blooms in summer. Plants are capable of growing to 1.2m (4ft) in their first season and then 1.8-2.4m (6-8ft) in subsequent years. The first tree lily was developed in the USA by American botanist Robert Griesbach, who selected tall varieties of Oriental lily and crossed them with trumpet lilies of similar stature. The resultant hybrids, dubbed Orienpet lilies in the USA, boasted the height and scent of both parents, along with the range of colours found with trumpet lilies, and the hardiness, large blooms and patterned flowers of Oriental lilies.

Grow Shallots

Shallots are prized for their delicate and complex flavour and can be cooked in curries, stews and stir-fries, or else be chopped raw into dressings and salads. Loved by foodies, shallots are easy to grow from sets (baby bulbs). Plant in the ground and they'll grow rapidly, providing a clump of up to ten full-sized bulbs by the end of summer.

HOW TO PLANT

Make small holes in the ground, 15cm (6in) apart, and plant each shallot set with the pointy nose of the bulb just poking above the surface. Leave a 30cm (12in) gap between rows. Firm the soil around the bulbs with your fingers and water well. Birds might pull up the bulbs after planting, so check regularly and re-firm the soil if necessary.

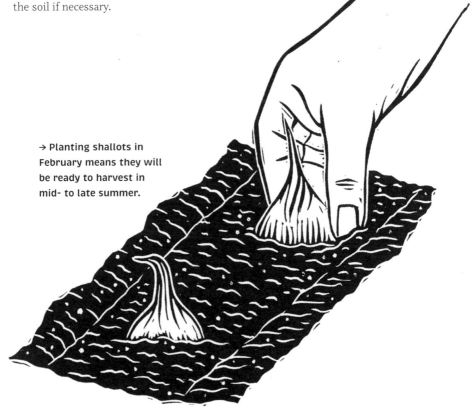

→ Planting shallots in February means they will be ready to harvest in mid- to late summer.

AFTERCARE

Water during dry spells and keep on top of weeds - spreading a layer of garden compost, 5cm (2in) deep, around plants will prevent weed seeds germinating. Give the plants a dose of general liquid fertilizer every four weeks before lightly feeding with sulphate of potash in June. This will help plump up the bulbs and improve flavour.

HARVESTING

Bulbs are ready for harvesting in mid- to late summer, once the foliage starts to wilt and turn brown. Prise clumps carefully from the ground, split them into individual bulbs and remove as much soil as possible. Allow the shallots to dry in the sun until the outer skin is papery. If the weather is wet, stand them on a wire rack indoors.

STORING

Shallots can be eaten immediately but they will keep for six months or more if stored in a cool, dry, dark and airy place such as a shed or garage. Either arrange a single layer on the base of a wicker tray or wooden fruit box, or stash them in a net bag and suspend from a hook.

THREE GREAT SHALLOT VARIETIES TO TRY

1 **'Golden Gourmet'** - large, round, golden-skinned bulbs have pink-tinged, white flesh with a mild taste.

2 **'Hermine'** - bred in France, the subtly flavoured, white-skinned bulbs contrast well with bright green foliage.

3 **'Vigarmor'** - a banana-shaped variety from France, with attractive, copper-coloured skin and pinky white flesh.

A POTTED HISTORY OF SHALLOTS

Nobody knows for certain where shallots originate but some historians think they were first cultivated in Central Asia, before making their way to India and the eastern Mediterranean region. They are believed to have been introduced into Britain by the Romans. Plant breeders have developed scores of different varieties, which vary enormously in size and shape, from small and round ones to chunky elongated types. The latter are often referred to as banana shallots and are known as echalions in France.

Time to Start Potatoes

Whether you like them mashed or crushed, sautéed or roasted, chipped, baked or boiled, now is the time to grow your own spuds by snapping up some seed potatoes. Despite their name, they aren't actually seeds but rather small tubers that will be ready for planting in spring, whether that's in the ground or in containers.

Seed potatoes are divided into groups based on when they are ready to harvest. First early or new potatoes can be dug up from late spring, while second early potatoes are usually ready in mid-summer. Maincrop potatoes can be lifted from late August into September.

Before planting seed potatoes it's best to force them to produce sprouts using a technique known as chitting, which encourages earlier and slightly larger harvests. Simply pop a seed potato into each cup in an egg box, ensuring that the part marked with most 'eyes', or indentations, is facing upward.

Place the egg box in a cool light spot, such as a spare room, porch or cold conservatory. Within a few days you'll notice tiny little shoots appear from the 'eyes', which will turn into short stubby sprouts. The potatoes will be ready for planting when the sprouts are 2.5cm (1in) long, a process that takes around six weeks or so.

FIVE SUPER SPUD VARIETIES TO TRY

1 **'Highland Burgundy Red'** - the long oval tubers of this maincrop potato are burgundy on the outside with unusual, two-tone, red and white flesh.

2 **'Pink Fir Apple'** - making its debut in 1850, the bumpy, pink and white tubers of this late maincrop variety are impossible to peel, so are best cooked whole.

3 **'Ratte'** - this heritage French variety of 1872 has long white tubers with a distinctive nutty taste and are delicious eaten as new potatoes or in salads.

4 **'Red Duke of York'** - discovered in the 1940s, this first early variety produces red-skinned spuds and has attractive green foliage that's flushed with purple.

5 **'Kestrel'** - bred in Scotland and introduced in 1992, this second early variety has long, white tubers that are marked with distinctive violet-blue eyes.

↓ Chit seed potatoes by placing each tuber into the cup of an egg box, making sure the 'rose end' (the part with most eyes) is facing upward.

Plant a Fig Tree

Originating from the Middle East, figs (*Ficus*) may have an exotic air because of their provenance but it's possible to grow this delicacy in cooler climates. There are plenty of varieties that are hardy down to -10°C (14°F), and these can be planted in the ground now to provide armfuls of sweet sticky fruit for many years to come.

Due to their far-flung origins, fig trees need a warm, sunny and sheltered spot to produce a decent crop. They can be grown as multistemmed or standard trees in the open ground or containers. Another option is to train young plants as fans or espaliers against south-facing walls and fences.

If left to their own devices, many fig trees will happily ascend to 6m (20ft) or more, with a similar spread. Apart from blocking out light and taking up space, large trees bear most of their fruit on branches out of reach. The fruit also tends to suffer in quality as bigger trees need loads of moisture and nutrients.

It's possible to limit the top growth of figs by restricting the spread of their roots. The traditional way of doing this is to construct a planting pit - a 60cm (24in)-square hole with a base of compacted rubble and sides lined with paving slabs. Fill the pit with soil-based potting compost or a mixture of normal soil and garden compost. Another option is to plant trees into 45-litre (10-gallon) fabric containers known as root control bags, which can then be sunk into the ground.

The inside of the bags is coated with copper, which stops vigorous root tips in their tracks, resulting in the production of more fibrous side roots.

WHEN DO FIGS PRODUCE FRUIT?

In warm, far-flung places, fig trees can produce three crops a year. Expect one good crop in cooler climates, from pea-sized baby fruit that appear in late spring. These swell over summer until they are ready to pick in August or September. Pick when the fruit droops down from the branch and is soft to the touch when gently squeezed.

THREE GREAT FIGS TO TRY

1 **'Brown Turkey'** - ideal in a cool-temperate climate, this popular variety from the 18th century has brown-skinned fruit with red flesh.

2 **'Rouge de Bordeaux'** - this old French variety is praised by gourmets for the fine flavour of its small purple fruit with red flesh.

3 **'Panachée'** - this 17th-century variety boasts green fruit heavily marked with yellow stripes, which give rise to its common name of tiger fig.

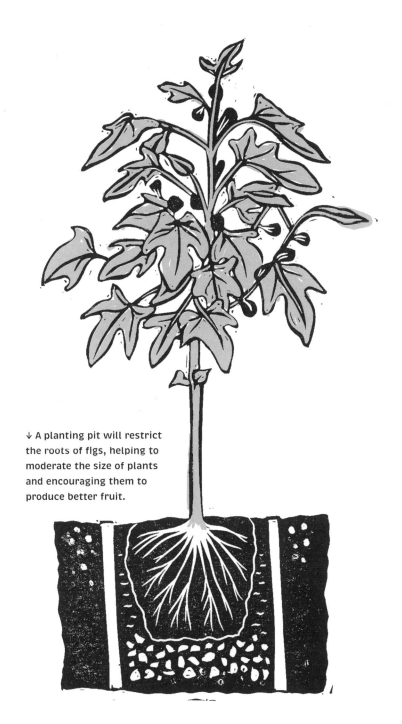

↓ A planting pit will restrict the roots of figs, helping to moderate the size of plants and encouraging them to produce better fruit.

Stop Slugs Eating Hostas

Hostas are martyrs to slugs and snails, which are drawn toward emerging shoots early in the season, and like to chomp holes in the leaves once they are fully unfurled. To prevent plants from being turned into lace doilies, it's best to put control measures in place as soon as shoots nose their way above ground in late winter, and to remain vigilant until summer. One way to deter slugs is to sprinkle organic slug pellets around vulnerable plants. Apart from killing the pests, these pellets give plants a boost by releasing iron and phosphate into the soil. Sadly, no hostas are slug-proof, but some seem to be more resistant to attack. Those with thick leaves or that are coated in a shiny waxy layer tend to remain unharmed, along with varieties that have blue leaves or a heavily corrugated surface. Among them are aptly named 'Invincible', 'Daybreak' and 'Halcyon'.

Trivia time

It is believed that the average British garden contains over 20,000 slugs and snails, with every cubic metre (cubic yard) housing around 200 slugs – about 90 percent of these gastropods live in the soil and emerge at night, during damp or wet weather.

Pest and Disease watch:
Grey Mould

Sometimes known as botrytis, this disease prospers in damp cold greenhouses in winter and results in a furry mould developing on leaves and stems. Prevent problems by watering only when compost is dry, and by opening doors and vents on mild days to allow fresh air to circulate. Remove leaves that show signs of infection and evict plants if badly contaminated.

Make a Crop Rotation Plan

It's important to avoid growing the same annual veggies in the same place each year, so put together a crop rotation plan. This helps to reduce the risk of pests and diseases establishing in the soil, and allows plants with similar feeding or watering needs to be treated together. One way of drawing up a crop rotation plan is to divide crops into three main groups: brassicas; root vegetables and salads; and peas, beans and fruiting vegetables. Grow each group in a separate bed or patch of soil this spring. Next year, grow brassicas in the space left by the peas, etc.; sow roots in the gap vacated by the brassicas; and plant peas in the remaining position. Rotate them again the year after. By year four, the vegetables will be back in their original positions.

Deal with Waterlogged Lawns

Lawns usually take wet weather in their stride, even if they have spent a week underwater. On the downside, the weight of surface water is likely to cause compaction, so wait until the lawn has dried out and then aerate with a hollow-tine tool. Replace lost nutrients by applying spring lawn fertilizer. Expect a different outcome with lawns that have been flooded for longer than a week. Over this time, water will have driven out air from the soil and the grass can turn a sickly yellow as roots are starved of oxygen. In this scenario, lift the dying turf and then re-seed or lay fresh turf from scratch.

Prevent Snow Damage to Conifers

Wayward branches on upright conifers can easily break under the weight of snow, causing damage to the rest of the plant. To prevent problems, completely cut out any offending branches. Alternatively, if removing shoots will spoil the conifer's shape, tie in branches by encircling the entire plant with garden twine. If any snow does settle, brush it off as soon as possible.

'There is no time like Spring,

When life's alive in everything'

(Christina Rossetti, *Spring*)

THE MONTH AT A GLANCE

- Divide clumps of congested perennials (see How to Divide Perennials, page 42).
- Move shrubs planted in the wrong place (see Move Shrubs, page 44).
- Remove old flowerheads from mophead and lacecap hydrangeas (see When Should I Prune Hydrangeas?, page 47).
- Cut back perennials left for winter interest (see Prune Plants Left for Winter Interest, page 47).
- Snip back stems of hardy fuchsias damaged by winter frosts.
- Topdress trees and shrubs in pots (see Revitalize Plants in Pots, page 46).
- Cut back leggy buddleias (see Maintain Buddleias, page 46).
- Remove the flowerheads from daffodils as they fade.
- Finish planting bare-root trees, shrubs and fruit before dormant plants break into leaf (see Bare-root Plants, page 216).
- Plant an apple tree (see Plant an Apple Tree, page 50).
- Ensure a bumper crop of blackcurrants by feeding plants with a high-nitrogen fertilizer.
- Lift, divide and replant unproductive clumps of rhubarb (see How to Grow Rhubarb, page 82).
- Sow seeds of peppers, tomatoes and cucumbers indoors (see Grow Peppers, page 58; Totally Tomatoes, page 60; Start Cucumbers, page 64).
- Plant asparagus crowns (see How To Grow Asparagus page 54).
- Sow basil seeds indoors (see It's Time to Sow Basil, page 52).
- Plant onion sets in the ground (see Plant Onion Sets, page 66).
- Lime the soil for growing brassicas (see Lime Soil for Brassicas, page 66).
- Spring clean greenhouses (see Get Greenhouses Winter-ready, page 215).
- Plant rhizomes of Indian shot plant (*Canna*) in pots indoors.

March

It can still be pretty cold at the start of March but it's time to celebrate the fact that winter is drawing to its inevitable close. Yay! This is a time of great activity for gardeners after a relatively quiet time outdoors during the past few months. All sorts of tender vegetables can now be sown indoors for planting out later in the season, while beds and borders need a bit of attention before they swing into action. Do keep an eye on the weather forecasts, though, as frosts are still just as likely as a spell of warm weather.

How to Divide Perennials

Over time, many herbaceous perennials will form large clumps that can engulf other plants, outgrow their allotted spot or become reluctant to flower. The good news is that it's easy to restore their vigour or to control their spread by using a tried-and-tested propagation technique known as division.

Division is a crude but effective way to increase your plant stock, and anyone can do it without needing specialist kit. All you require is a spade, a couple of forks, some secateurs and a sturdy old bread knife. A wheelbarrow is useful for moving gear around and holding plants steady as they are being divided.

As a crude rule of thumb, perennials that flower after Midsummer's Day (24 June) are suitable for dividing in spring, while those that bloom before this date are best left until autumn. However, many gardeners prefer to divide everything in spring because wet or cold weather later in the year can result in divided sections rotting.

There are several methods of physically dividing up clumps, depending on the root system of the plant. Aim to work as quickly as possible to prevent roots drying out and then replant at the previous depth in holes that are three times as wide as the divided section.

» THREE WAYS OF DIVIDING PERENNIALS «

1   Tackle asters, yarrow (*Achillea*) and plants with fibrous roots by lifting them from the ground and plunging two forks into the centre, back-to-back. Split in two by pushing the forks outward.

2   Plants with a loose network of roots, such as heucheras and hostas, are usually easy enough to tease apart by hand.

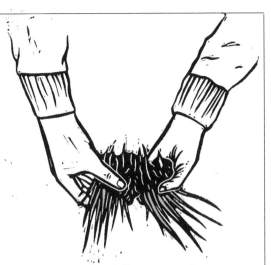

3   Perennials with thick sturdy roots need a bit of elbow grease. Place clumps of day lilies (*Hemerocallis*), red-hot pokers (*Kniphofia*) and delphiniums inside a wheelbarrow and slice up the rootball with a spade or else carve it into smaller pieces with a bread knife.

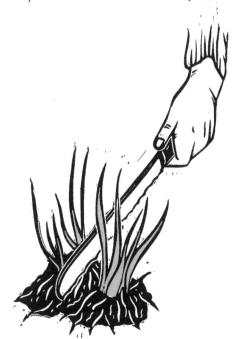

A WORD OF WARNING:

Not all perennials can be divided. Those with multiple stems that emanate from the crown of the plant or that produce long taproots are no-nos. This includes aconite (*Aconitum*), gypsophila, bleeding heart (*Lamprocapnos*) and lupin (*Lupinus*), along with ornamental thistles such as cirsium, globe thistle (*Echinops*) and sea holly (*Eryngium*).

Move Shrubs

Right shrub, wrong place? Don't worry, most shrubs that have been in the ground for five years or less are relatively easy to move from one part of the garden to a more favourable spot (the process is known by seasoned gardeners as transplanting). Older plants can be trickier to transplant but it is not impossible.

Most deciduous shrubs are best tackled between late October and March, while evergreens are best moved in October or April. Avoid shifting plants in summer, if at all possible. Being hoicked from the ground during hot dry weather is stressful for them, and they'll respond by wilting or shedding leaves.

» HOW TO DO IT «

1 Dig a circular trench, 30cm (12in) deep, around the shrub, using the spread of its branches as a guide to the appropriate diameter.

2 Undercut the core of soil with the aim of removing a large rootball - use the spade to slice in at a 45-degree angle, working around the base and gradually tunnelling underneath. It's inevitable that you will sever some roots during the process.

3 Lift the rootball and wrap it in a garden sheet to prevent the roots drying out.

4 Dig a new planting hole that's the same depth as the soil rootball and about twice as wide.

5 Lower the rootball into position and fill gaps around the outside with soil, firming down as you go to eliminate air pockets. Water well.

↓ When moving a shrub aim to dig out as a large a rootball as possible. If you come across any really thick roots that are difficult to sever with a spade, use a hand-held pruning saw.

Maintain Buddleias

If you turn a blind eye to butterfly bushes (*Buddleja davidii*) they will soar upward, holding their flowers well out of sight. In order to keep them at a reasonable height, trim them twice a year. In early spring, cut back all shoots hard, to leave two buds above the darker older growth - each plant will respond with a flush of fresh stems that will carry flowers in summer. In autumn, remove the tips of stems that flowered in early autumn, to prevent them being rocked about in windy weather. If you grow dwarf buddleias, prune down to 30cm (12in) for the first few years after planting. After this, cut branches back to two buds above the previous year's growth.

EXCEPTION TO THE RULE

Not all buddleias like being pruned in early spring. *Buddleja alternifolia* is a weeping shrub that produces its purple flowers on older wood, so trimming early in the year would result in a poor display in late spring and early summer. Instead, cut back branches immediately after flowering to improve and maintain the plant's shape.

Revitalize Plants in Pots

Plants in pots soon run out of steam when they exhaust the nutrients in their compost, so give them a pick-me-up by topdressing with fresh compost. To do this, carefully scrape off as much of the old compost from the surface as you can without damaging any of the roots beneath. About 2.5cm (1in) is ideal. Replace with fresh compost mixed with a handful of controlled-release fertilizer granules to keep your plants growing strong and healthily for the next few months.

A POTTED HISTORY OF BUDDLEIAS

The butterfly bush (*Buddleja davidii*) is a common sight on wasteland, railway embankments and even growing out of the sides of old buildings. Yet this ubiquitous plant is not a native to our shores. It actually arrived here from China in 1896 and became a popular garden plant thanks to its colourful, honey-scented summer flowers. It was discovered to be a prolific self-seeder, and by 1922 it had gone rogue, with the first garden escapee recorded at Harlech in north Wales. During the Second World War it was dubbed the bomb-site plant because seedlings quickly colonized areas damaged during the Blitz.

Prune Plants Left for Winter Interest

The old seedheads of perennials provide sculptural interest over winter, but by early spring they've outstayed their welcome. Nothing looks worse than a jungle of tatty stems, so take a pair of secateurs and cut them all down to ground level. After pruning, give the soil a boost by mulching with a 7.5cm (3in) layer of garden compost, leafmould or well-rotted manure.

When Should I Prune Hydrangeas?

It's a question that has long vexed gardeners and the answer is...it depends on what kind of hydrangea you have.

Cultivars of *Hydrangea macrophylla* are divided into two groups: mophead and lacecap. The flowerheads of mophead types, which look like 1950s-style floral bathing caps, are best left on plants over winter and trimmed off in early spring, when you cut back to a pair of strong buds. Prune lacecap hydrangeas, with their flat flowerheads surrounded by a ring of pretty florets, in a similar way, once plants have finished flowering in autumn. After deadheading, remove about one-quarter of the older branches if plants are congested.

Varieties of *H. paniculata* are best pruned in early spring, and they respond well to tougher treatment - create a low framework by cutting back the stems close to ground level. Maintain the attractive shape of oak-leaved hydrangeas (*H. quercifolia*) by pruning them immediately after flowering.

← In early spring, remove the old flowerheads from mophead hydrangeas, cutting just above a pair of buds.

Common Leaf Shapes

The leaf shapes of plants vary considerably and these have been given their own names to make identification easier. Here are a few common ones that you might come across while reading plant labels and descriptions when shopping for new specimens:

arrow-shaped (sagittate)

heart-shaped (cordate)

pinnate (pinnata)

rounded (rotundifolia)

lance-shaped (lanceolate)

palmate (palmate)

spear-shaped (hastate)

strap-shaped (ensiform)

Grow Pears

Descending from a wild species (Pyrus communis) that's native to Central and Eastern Europe, along with parts of southwest Asia, pears are treated in a similar way to apples. There are thought to be around 3,000 different pears worldwide with almost 200 varieties available to buy from nurseries in the UK. Some are self-fertile and will produce fruit without any assistance, but others need to grow in the vicinity of another pear to ensure the flowers are pollinated. Like apples, varieties are grafted onto rootstocks that govern their vigour and eventual height. The five main pear rootstocks are: Quince C (2.4-3m/8-10ft), Quince A (3-3.5m/10-12ft), Quince BA29 (3.5m/12ft), Pyrodwarf (over 5m/16ft), Pyrus communis (over 6m/20ft).

Plant an Apple Tree

Picking an apple straight from the tree is one of life's greatest pleasures during late summer and autumn, but with so many varieties available, choosing what to grow can cause some serious head scratching. One solution is to do a taste test of varieties at a local apple fair or to pick a heritage apple that was raised locally to where you live.

BUYING PLANTS

Bare-root trees are generally available from November until April. Some garden centres stock a few different varieties, but for a greater choice check out the ranges offered online by specialist fruit nurseries. Container-grown plants are more expensive to buy but are available all year round.

Before buying an apple tree, make sure it's growing on a rootstock that suits the size of your garden. If grown on their own roots, apples become too large or produce disappointing crops. To overcome this, apple trees are propagated by grafting, where the shoot of one variety is joined to the roots, or rootstock, of another. This controls the growth rate and the eventual size of the tree. The six main apple rootstocks in order of size of tree they produce are: M27 (1.2-1.8m/4-6ft), M9 (1.8-3m/6-10ft), M26 (2.4-3.6m/8-12ft), MM106 (2.4-4.5m/8-14ft), MM111 (4-4.5m/13-15ft), M25 (over 4.5m/15ft).

HOW TO GROW

Apple trees can be grown in a number of ways. Ready-trained espalier and cordons are ideal where space is tight as they can be grown against walls and fences. Alternatively, trees on M27 and M9 rootstocks can be grown in 45-60cm (18-24in)-wide pots. If space is no problem, grow a freestanding bush or standard apple tree.

WHERE TO PLANT

Plant apple trees in well-drained soil and full sun. As they generally produce blossom between late April and mid-May, choose a sheltered spot so the flowers aren't damaged by frost. Pollination is also carried out by insects, which will be put off by strong winds in more open parts of the garden.

WHAT NEXT

It's best to remove all flowers from newly planted apples in spring to allow energy to be put into the development of roots and branches. Most varieties will start to produce fruit in their third to fourth year, but this does vary and some will bear fruit from their second year onward.

TEN GREAT HERITAGE APPLE VARIETIES FROM AROUND THE BRITISH ISLES

1 'Ashmead's Kernel' (Gloucestershire, England, introduced 1700).

2 'Bess Pool' (Nottinghamshire, England, 1820s).

3 'D'Arcy Spice' (Essex, England, 1785).

4 'Diamond Apple' (Gwynedd, Wales, 1850).

5 'Hawthornden' (Midlothian, Scotland, 1780).

6 'Irish Peach' (County Sligo, Ireland, 1820).

7 'Lady Henniker' (Suffolk, England, 1873).

8 'Manks Codlin' (Isle of Man, 1815).

9 'Pitmaston Pine Apple' (Worcestershire, England, 1785).

10 'Stirling Castle' (Stirlingshire, Scotland, 1831).

A POTTED HISTORY OF CULTIVATED APPLES

Cultivated apples (*Malus domestica*) were introduced to Britain by the Romans. Botanists used to think they were descended from wild trees with small, sour fruit, but modern DNA analysis has instead revealed them to be the offspring of *M. sieversii*, a tree with larger, sweeter fruit found in the Tian Shan mountains between China, Kazakhstan and Kyrgyzstan.

DID YOU KNOW ?

Apple Records was set up by The Beatles in 1968. The printed labels on the A-side of UK releases featured a bright green 'Granny Smith', while the reverse was illustrated by a cross-section of the fruit. George Harrison's *Extra Texture* album from 1975 featured a well-eaten apple core on the label.

It's Time to Sow Basil

Basil is a kitchen staple, and its aromatic leaves are added fresh to dishes like salads and pizzas, used to flavour oils and vinegars, or pounded up to make sauces. Despite its association with Italian cuisine, basil actually originates from India and tropical regions of Asia - a variety known as holy basil is considered sacred by Hindus and is grown outside temples and homes. Ready-grown basil plants are widely available in spring but they're very easy to grow from seed.

SOWING SEEDS

Fill a small pot with seed compost, level and tap to settle. Lightly firm with the bottom of another pot, and then thinly scatter seed on top - only sow one or two more seeds than you need in case of losses. Cover with a fine layer of vermiculite, water and label. Place in a heated propagator. Remove the pots once the seeds have germinated and stand them on a light windowsill.

LOOKING AFTER BASIL

When the seedlings are about 2.5cm (1in) tall, pot them on into individual 7.5cm (3in) pots filled with multipurpose potting compost. Make sure the leaves are just above the surface of the soil, gently firm in and water. When roots start to poke through the drainage holes at the bottom of containers, move the basil plants into 12cm (5in) pots. At the end of May, after hardening off (see page 94) slip the basil plants into decorative outer containers and place in a sunny spot outside. Plants will grow quickly, so pot on regularly to avoid a check to growth.

HARVESTING

The more you harvest the leaves, the more basil plants produce further foliage. Take what you need by pinching out the growing tips of branches, leaving a small stub behind. Apart from giving you lots of tasty leaves to use in the kitchen, the basil plant will respond by growing back bigger and bushier. Result!

FIVE GREAT BASIL VARIETIES TO TRY

1 'Genovese' - a classic Italian variety with lovely aromatic leaves.

2 'Horapha' - is used in Thai food and has leaves with a sweet liquorice flavour.

3 'Mrs Burns' - leaves have a distinctive lime kick.

4 'Purple Ruffles' - large, dark purple, crinkled leaves with deeply toothed margins.

5 'Red Rubin' - bronze leaves with a sweet aroma and flavour.

Making Pesto

This aromatic herb is famed as the main ingredient of pesto, a verdant Italian sauce that has been eaten for centuries. To make 250ml (8 fl. oz) of sauce, toast 50g (1½oz) pine nuts in a dry pan and add to a food processor with 80g (2½oz) basil leaves, 50g (1½oz) Parmesan cheese, 150ml (5 fl. oz) olive oil and two garlic cloves. Blitz until smooth.

For really authentic pesto, grow the basil variety 'Tigullio', which boasts large, slightly curled leaves. It is grown commercially for pesto in the fields of Liguria, northwest Italy.

**Name explain:
Forsythia**

Known for their cheery yellow flowers, forsythias are a group of spring-flowering shrubs that were named after Scottish gardener William Forsyth (1737-1804). A curator of the Chelsea Physic Garden and founding member of the Horticultural Society (now the Royal Horticultural Society), he was the great-great-great-great grandfather of the late TV showman Bruce Forsyth.

DID YOU KNOW ?

In the 16th century, influential physicians eyed basil with suspicion. Some believed that the mere hint of the aromatic leaves would lead to someone's brains being infested with scorpions, while the author of The Herball (1597), John Gerard, held the view that if you chewed some leaves and spat them out, worms would spontaneously appear from the ground.

How to Grow Asparagus

Asparagus has long been considered an aphrodisiac. Way back in 1597, herbalist John Gerard wrote that eating asparagus was 'thought to increase seed, and stir up lust'. Across the English Channel in the 19th century, French bridegrooms were served asparagus at their wedding reception to get them in the mood for love.

Being a potent source of potassium, folic acid and fibre, and containing vitamins A, B and C, asparagus spears aren't just good for you - they also have a delectable taste and succulent texture that make them hot property with foodies during their growing season, from late April to the end of June.

This gourmet veg thrives in a sunny, sheltered spot and prefers rich, well-drained soil - it will perform poorly in heavy clay or shady places. For a worthwhile crop you need plenty of space, such as a raised bed, allotment or dedicated veg patch. Unfortunately, it's not really suitable for growing in containers.

Asparagus can be grown from seeds, but you'll have to wait at least three years before there's anything worth picking. It's far easier to start from dormant plants, known as crowns. One-year-old crowns will provide spears within two years, while two-year-old crowns can be harvested after a year.

MYTHS AND LEGENDS

In Greek mythology, Theseus killed a bandit called Sinis and hunted for the man's daughter, Perigune. She hid from the mythical king in a thicket of thorny asparagus stems and vowed never to chop the plants down if they concealed her. Descendants of Perigune formed a colony in Anatolia, where asparagus was revered and never cut back.

DID YOU KNOW ?

Asparagus was highly prized by the ancient Romans. Emperor Augustus (63BC - AD14) established the asparagus fleet of ships to transport the harvested crop from source to the dining tables of the nobility in Rome.

Good preparation is essential. Dig a trench that is 20cm (8in) deep and 30cm (12in) wide. Spread some well-rotted manure along the bottom and cover with a 5cm (2in) layer of soil. Make a soil ridge, 10cm (4in) high, down the centre of the trench and place the crowns on top, 30cm (12in) apart, spreading the roots evenly down each side of the ridge. Carefully cover the crowns with about 5cm (2in) of sieved soil; then water. Leave 45cm (18in) between subsequent trenches and stagger the asparagus crowns between adjacent rows. As the stems develop during the season, cover with more seived soil. Aim to completely fill the trench with soil by autumn.

It may be tempting, but don't pick any spears from newly planted crowns during their first growing season. Let the plants establish underground by allowing the stems to extend upward. Cut the 1.5m (5ft)-tall, ferny fronds down to just above ground level when they start to turn yellow in autumn. Keep the bed free of weeds and spread some general fertilizer granules over the ground the next spring.

If you planted two-year-old crowns, you'll be able to harvest stems for about eight weeks from around April. Those with younger crowns will have to wait another year, although it won't hurt to take the odd one to sample.

A POTTED HISTORY OF ASPARAGUS

Native to parts of the eastern Mediterranean and West Asia, wild asparagus (*Asparagus officinalis*) can be found in a range of habitats, including meadows, hillsides and sand dunes. The edible young shoots grow rapidly into towering stems that are clothed with fern-like foliage. Asparagus has been cultivated as a food crop for over 2,000 years and was first grown in Britain during the 16th century.

CUTTING SPEARS

Harvest asparagus spears when they are about 18cm (7in) long, using a serrated knife to slice 2.5cm (1in) below the surface of the soil. Remember to harvest the spears every few days, but stop cutting in mid-June, to allow plants to build up their energy for the following year.

FIVE GREAT ASPARAGUS VARIETIES TO TRY

1 **'Connover's Colossal'** - a high-yielding variety with green spears and purple tips.

2 **'Gijnlim'** - bred in Holland, the green spears are thick and juicy.

3 **'Guelph Millennium'** - produces heavy crops of purple-tipped spears.

4 **'Pacific Purple'** - developed in New Zealand, the purple spears are very sweet.

5 **'Burgundine'** - the low fibre content of the red-purple shoots makes this variety ideal for eating raw.

'In garden arrangement, as in all other kinds of decorative work, one has not only to acquire a knowledge of what to do, but also to gain some wisdom in perceiving what it is well to let alone.'

Gertrude Jekyll

↓ Plant asparagus in a sunny, sheltered spot with well-drained soil. Set crowns 30cm (12in) apart on ridges, helping to prevent waterlogging.

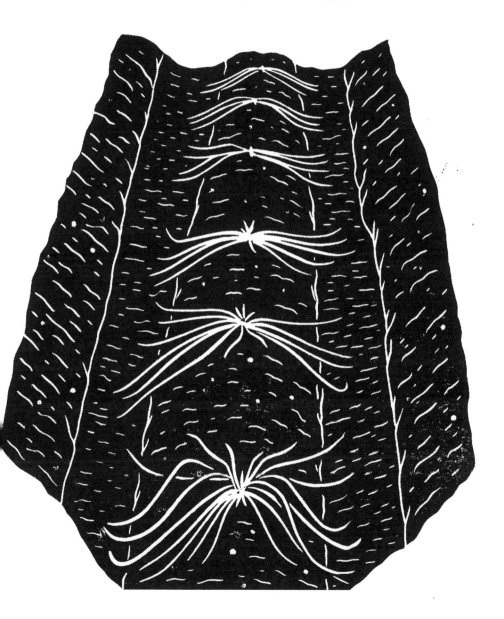

Grow Peppers

It doesn't matter whether you're a self-confirmed chilli head or prefer the mild taste of sweet peppers, both types are very easy to grow from seeds. Despite the difference in flavour, chilli and sweet peppers both originate from *Capsicum annuum*, a plant indigenous to Mexico, Central America and northern South America.

» SOWING SEEDS «

1   Fill a 7.5cm (3in) pot with seed compost, level and tap to settle. Lightly firm the compost with the bottom of another pot.

2   Scatter seed thinly on top of the compost. Most will germinate, so sow only a few more than you need in case of losses.

3   Cover with a fine layer of vermiculite, water using a watering can with a rose attachment to avoid dislodging the seed, and then put in a heated propagator.

4   After the seeds have germinated, place the pot on a light windowsill or in a heated greenhouse.

5   When the seedlings are 2.5cm (1in) tall, transplant each one into a 7.5cm (3in) pot filled with multipurpose potting compost.

6   Move plants into larger pots when the roots start poking through the drainage holes.

DID YOU KNOW ?

The mascot for the 1986 World Cup held in Mexico was a sombrero-wearing jalapeño pepper called Pique.

THE HOT CHILLI PEPPER LIST

○ **Anaheim** - 500-2,500 SHU

○ **Poblano** - 1,000-2,000 SHU

○ **Jalapeño** - 2,500-8,000 SHU

○ **Arbol** - 15,000-30,000 SHU

○ **Cayenne** - 30,000-50,000 SHU

○ **Thai** - 50,000-100,000 SHU

○ **Scotch bonnet** - 100,000-350,000 SHU

○ **Ghost** - 1 million SHU

○ **'Carolina Reaper'** - 2.2 million SHU

○ **US police-grade pepper spray** - 5.3 million SHU

WHAT NEXT...

Move plants outside when there's no longer any danger of frost, which is usually in late May or early June. Either plant individually into 20cm (8in)-diameter pots or arrange three pepper plants, side by side, in a grow-bag. Alternatively, plant directly into the ground, spacing the pepper 45cm (18in) apart. Support the stems with bamboo canes.

LOOKING AFTER THEM

Water plants regularly, especially in hot weather, and start feeding when flowers appear - feed every two weeks with a high-potash fertilizer until fruits have been picked. Harvest the fruit when ripe, removing each pepper with a sharp knife or pair of secateurs. Picking regularly will encourage the plants to produce even more peppers.

WHAT'S THE SCOVILLE SCALE?

The spicy heat of chilli peppers is caused by a compound called capsaicin. The amount varies from mild to something that will bring tears to your eyes, depending on the type of pepper. Their pungency is measured by Scoville Heat Units (SHU) on the Scoville Heat Scale, invented by American pharmacist Wilbur Scoville in 1912.

Totally Tomatoes

Mention the word tomato and most people will think of a red, round and juicy fruit that's a bit smaller than a golf ball. Yet there are hundreds of different tomatoes in the world, with fruit that differs in size, shape and colour. There are spherical, pear-, sausage- and egg-shaped tomatoes, with fruit measuring anywhere from the size of a pea to around 15cm (6in) across. Many are a shade of red, but there are also white, yellow, green, orange, pink, purple and near black ones. Some are striped or speckled with a different colour.

Even the taste can vary considerably between varieties, depending on the sugar and organic acid content. They vary in taste between strong and mild, sweet and acidic, to those that possess a perfectly balanced flavour. Some have a more complex flavour with smoky, citrus and spicy hints.

To enjoy your own tasty tomatoes, sow some seeds indoors in early spring and they'll germinate readily. The vigorous young plants will be ready for planting outdoors in late spring and will romp away in a sunny, sheltered spot, rewarding you with masses of fruit from mid-summer until the first frosts.

WHERE TO GROW

Bush tomatoes can be planted in a sunny spot outdoors or in 20cm (8in)-wide containers - compact types are ideal in hanging baskets. Cordon types are ideal in greenhouses or large containers.

It's possible to grow three different tomato varieties in a single grow-bag. Prepare the bag by kneading it to break up any lumps and then cut out three wide planting slots in the top. To give plants more growing space, cut the bottoms off three 20cm (8in)-wide pots and then 'screw' them into the holes. Add compost to each pot and plant a young tomato plant in it.

HEALTH BENEFITS OF TOMATOES

Tomatoes are a bona fide superfood. They are a good source of vitamins C, A and E, along with minerals like potassium, iron and calcium. They also contain lycopene, a compound that is believed to have the potential to reduce the risk of cardiovascular disease - the highest concentrations of lycopene can be found in red-fruited varieties.

1   Fill a 7.5cm (3in) pot with seed compost, level and tap to settle. Lightly firm the compost with the bottom of another pot and then scatter a few seeds on top. Most will germinate, so sow only two or three more seeds than you need in case of losses. Cover with a fine layer of vermiculite, water and pop in a label. Place the pot in a heated propagator or cover with a clear polythene bag, secured with a rubber band.

2   After germination, place the pot on a bright windowsill. When the seedlings are about 2.5cm (1in) tall, separate them carefully and plant each one in a 7.5cm (3in) pot filled with peat-free potting compost. Move young plants into larger pots when roots start poking out of the drainage holes in the base. Repeat the process as necessary.

3   Stake the stems of cordon tomato varieties with short bamboo support sticks when they are about 15cm (6in) tall, to encourage upright growth and to prevent flopping.

4   Tomatoes are ready to head outdoors when they've been hardened off (see page 94) and there's no longer any danger from frost.

5   Water regularly, ensuring the compost never dries out completely, and feed plants every week with liquid tomato food once the first flower truss appears.

DID YOU KNOW ?

Twenty thousand people descend upon the Spanish town of Buñol every August for the tomato-throwing festival of *La Tomatina*. Held since 1945, the giant food fight lasts an hour with around 150 tonnes of ripe fruit launched by participants.

TWO MAIN GROWTH HABITS

Tomato varieties fall into two main camps: bush (sometimes called determinate) and cordon (indeterminate). The latter need supporting with a cane and are grown as a single-stemmed plant with sideshoots removed, while bush types have more of a sprawling habit and require pruning only to keep them within bounds.

DIFFERENT TOMATO TYPES

Tomato varieties fall into different groups depending on their shape and size:

- **currant** - super-sweet, pea-sized fruit up to 1cm (½in) across;
- **cherry** - small, spherical fruit that weigh in at 10-20g (⅓-⅔oz);
- **salad** - medium-sized, globe-shaped fruit;
- **plum** - elongated fruit that is ideal for making soups and sauces;
- **beefsteak** - large tomatoes that weigh 180-250g (6-9oz) each.

FIVE WEIRD AND WONDERFUL TOMATO VARIETIES

1 **'Ananas Noire'** - flattened red fruit with green, red and yellow flesh.

2 **'Green Sausage'** - banana-shaped, yellow fruit adorned with green stripes.

3 **'Ol' German Pink'** - whopping fruit that can weigh 500g (1.1lb) with very few seeds.

4 **'Purple Calabash'** - a beefsteak type with heavily ribbed, purple-red fruit.

5 **'Reisetomate'** - bizarre fruit that resembles a cluster of cherry tomatoes.

> Word buster:
> **Petrichor**
>
> The distinctive, pleasant, earthy scent that fills the air after the first few drops of rain fall on dry soil or ground.

TRAINING TOMATOES

Bush tomatoes simply need vigorous shoots pruning to keep them within their allotted space.

The aim with cordon varieties is to create a single-stemmed plant. Support with a stake or stout cane, securing the main stem every 10cm (4in) with soft twine. Remove sideshoots that form inleaf joints when they are about 2.5cm (1in) long, snapping them off with a swift downward movement. After the first trusses of tiny fruit appear, strip away leaves to allow light and air to reach them. When the plant has produced four sets of flowering trusses, pinch out the growing tip to ensure all of the plant's energy goes into producing fruit.

↑ Snap sideshoots off cordon tomatoes as soon as they are large enough to handle.

Start Cucumbers

Back in the 18th century, many folk thought cucumbers were poisonous but in the 21st century we know the exact opposite to be true. These summer salad veggies are a source of vitamin K and also contain lignans, which are thought to reduce the risk of heart disease. Made up of 96 percent water, cucumbers are naturally low in calories.

There are scores of different varieties, split into two main groups: greenhouse and outdoors. The former prefers warm sheltered conditions, while the latter cucumbers are tougher and require insect activity to ensure good pollination. Some cucumbers are happy indoors or outside. Check the variety description before buying.

» HOW TO SOW & GROW «

1   Sow two seeds on their side, 1cm (½in) deep, in 7.5cm (3in) pots filled with seed compost. Place in a windowsill propagator (or cover with a clear polythene bag) until the seeds have germinated.

2   Pull up the weakest seedlings when they are 5cm (2in) tall. Put the pots in a warm light place.

3   When young plants have developed three or four leaves, move them into 25cm (10in) pots of good-quality compost.

4   Plant greenhouse varieties into even larger pots or grow-bags inside heated structures. Wait until May if the greenhouse doesn't have a heater. Train the main stem up a vertical wire or cane. Snip off the growing point when it reaches the roof to encourage flowering shoots below. Pinch out the tips of these sideshoots two leaves beyond each fruit. If sideshoots don't have any flowers or fruit, cut the ends once they are 60cm (24in) long. Cucumbers will thrive if you keep the humidity high within the greenhouse by watering the floor in the morning during sunny weather.

    OR

    Plant cucumbers outdoors once they've been hardened off (see page 94) and there's no longer any danger of frost, usually by late May or early June. Plant directly into the ground and train the stems up a tall cane. Alternatively, raise plants individually in 30cm (12in) pots or place two in a grow-bag.

5   Keep plants happy by feeding them every 10-14 days with a balanced liquid fertilizer, changing this to a high-potash feed once the first fruits start to set.

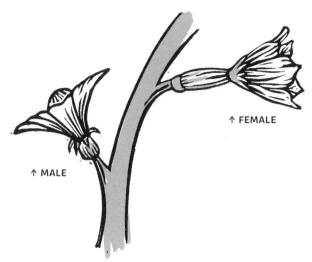

↑ FEMALE

↑ MALE

MALE & FEMALE CUCUMBER FLOWERS

Most cucumber varieties produce male and female flowers: female flowers have a baby fruit growing behind them, while male flowers have a plain stalk. Outdoor cucumbers need both present for insects to pollinate, but indoor types require the male flowers removing to prevent cross-pollination, leading to bitter fruit.

THREE COOL CUCUMBER VARIETIES TO TRY

1 'Burpless Tasty Green' - an old variety that produces 25cm (10in)-long fruit with dark green skin and crisp, refreshing, white flesh. Grow indoors or outdoors.

2 'Crystal Apple' - first sold in Australia back in the 1930s, this produces pale yellow-skinned, apple-shaped fruits with white flesh. Grow indoors or outdoors.

3 'White Wonder' - developed in the United States back in the late 19th century, this forms 20cm (8in)-long, chunky fruit with pale ivory skin. Grow indoors or outdoors.

DID YOU KNOW ?

Dr Samuel Johnson was one of the 18th-century's greatest polymaths but he harboured a deep, irrational and strong dislike of cucumbers. They are given short shrift in his *Dictionary of the English Language*, where they are described as 'name of a plant, and fruit of that plant'. Johnson later commented to his friend and biographer James Boswell that 'a cucumber should be well sliced, and dressed with pepper and vinegar, and then thrown out, as good for nothing.'

Plant Onion Sets

It's possible to raise onions from seed but it's quicker and easier to start them off from 'sets', essentially marble-sized bulbs that were harvested, dried and stored the previous year. These can be planted directly into well-prepared ground in March and April. Make a hole with a dibber, pop in a bulb and replace some soil, firming the miniature onion in place with your fingers - the pointy end should just be peeking above the surface. Leave 10cm (4in) between bulbs and, if you're planting on an allotment, allow 30cm (12in) between rows. Keep the ground weed-free to ensure the onions have plenty of space to swell. Water if the weather is dry and give an occasional feed with a general liquid fertilizer. The bulbs will be ready for harvesting in summer, once the leaves turn brown and collapse.

Lime Soil for Brassicas

Cauliflowers, kale, Brussels sprouts, broccoli and other members of the cabbage family are vulnerable to clubroot, a fungal disease that is more prevalent in acidic soil, causing stunted growth and wilting. If you have acidic soil and are planning on growing any brassicas, it's a good idea to increase its alkalinity with garden lime (calcium carbonate). Put on gloves and goggles, and then sprinkle across the soil surface - the amount you apply depends on soil type, so follow the instructions on the packet. Rake the golden lime gently into the surface.

Pest and Disease Watch: Powdery Mildew

This common fungal disease attacks a wide range of ornamental and edible plants, causing a white powdery substance to cover leaves, stems and flowers. As the disease takes hold, the leaves will become distorted and infected parts take on a purple-brown hue. Leaves might drop prematurely and plants sometimes die. It is most common where the soil is dry but the air around the plants is humid. If plants have powdery mildew, prune out infected parts and clear away fallen leaves to prevent spores overwintering. It is possible to treat badly affected plants with fungicide. Avoid problems such as this disease by keeping plants well-watered (but never water from above).

CAPITAL CITIES OF THE BRITISH ISLES CAPTURED IN PLANT NAMES

- *Betula* 'Edinburgh'
- *Epimedium wushanense* 'Cardiff Star'
- *Malus domestica* 'London Pippin'
- *Narcissus* 'Belfast Queen'
- *Rosa* DUBLIN BAY

Trivia time

In 1971, the humble daffodil was given a chilling transformation by the makers of the television programme *Doctor Who*. In a four-part serial called Terror of the Autons, the Doctor's arch enemy, the Master, tried to destroy the human race with faux daffodils that sprayed a plastic film over people's faces, causing them to suffocate. The scary storyline was controversial at the time and was criticized in the House of Lords by Labour peer Baroness Bacon, who said: 'Many children must have gone to bed and had nightmares.'

'When April scatters charms of primrose gold

Among the copper leaves in thickets old,

And singing skylarks from the meadows rise,

To twinkle like black stars in sunny skies'

(W H Davies, *April's Charms*)

THE MONTH AT A GLANCE

- Prune shrubs damaged by frosts (see Prune Frost-damaged Shrubs page 78).
- Pinch out the growing shoots of bedding plants to encourage bushier growth.
- Install supports for perennials (see Support Perennials, page 84).
- Water newly planted trees, shrubs and other plants during dry spells.
- Plant sweet pea seeds (see Start Sweet Peas, page 74).
- Set strawberry plants in the ground (see Scrumptious Strawberries, page 80).
- Tie new stems of raspberries and other cane fruits to supports (see Grow Raspberries, page 227).
- Plant rhubarb crowns (see How to Grow Rhubarb, page 82).
- Sow carrot seeds (see How to Grow Carrots, page 86).
- Plant first early, second early and maincrop seed potatoes (see Time to Start Potatoes, page 34).
- Sow pea seeds (see Start Peas from Seed, page 89).
- Sow chive seeds (see Grow Chives, page 88).
- Create a new lawn from turf (see Lay a Lawn, page 192).
- Feed mature lawns (see Deal with Waterlogged Lawns, page 39).
- Aerate, feed, scarify and repair lawns (see Get Your Lawns into Shape for Summer, page 70).
- Remove blanketweed and algae from ponds (see Improve Your Pond, page 78).
- Lift and divide aquatic perennials (see Improve Your Pond, page 78).
- Add new plants to ponds (see Improve Your Pond, page 78).
- Cool down greenhouses on warm days (see Cool Down Greenhouses, page 78).
- Plant up hanging baskets (see Make Hanging Baskets, page 76).
- Control box tree moths and caterpillars (see Pest and Disease Watch: Box Tree Moth, page 91).
- Repaint or treat wooden garden furniture with preservative.

April

It might be famed for its showers, but the weather
in April is changeable, with downpours, sunny
spells and late frosts all possible. In fact, you can't
even rule out a surprise snow flurry. Whatever
happens with the weather, there's plenty to keep
you busy in the garden. Pots of seedlings will be
jostling for space indoors, the soil is perfect for
sowing many outdoor crops, and lawns require
attention to prepare them for summer. A word of
warning: warmer weather inevitably means the
arrival of pests, so be on your guard.

Get Your Lawn into Shape for Summer

Whatever its size, a lawn sets a garden off to perfection, acting as a foil to beds, borders and other displays, while providing a versatile surface that can be used for eating, relaxing or playing. Unfortunately, poor weather over winter can leave a lawn looking a bit washed out, so give it some attention to prepare it for summer.

REMOVE THATCH

The thick layer of dead grass that forms on the surface of the lawn is known as thatch, and it prevents grass from growing healthily, impedes drainage and stops air from reaching the roots, thereby creating the perfect conditions for diseases to flourish. The troublesome brown material is clearly visible under the grass, and you'll also know if your lawn is affected if it's spongy to walk on. Remove thatch by drawing a spring-tine rake backward and forward lightly over the lawn – a technique known as scarifying.

TREAT COMPACTION

Heavy foot traffic on grass paths, entrances to lawns or a strip where the dog patrols will lead to soil particles being squashed together. As a result of this compaction, growth is weak and drainage impeded so much that puddles remain after a downpour. Treat these by plunging a garden fork into the ground every 10cm (4in) across the affected area. Finish by spreading a sandy topdressing (a mixture of sand and topsoil) over the surface, working it into the holes with a broom.

FEED LAWNS

Perk up tired lawns with a granular or liquid fertilizer. These are higher in nitrogen than those marked for use in autumn, and they help sallow grass turn green and encourage it to grow thickly. As well as fertilizers, there are combined lawn weed, feed and moss killers, and those supplemented with beneficial bacteria or fungi to promote healthy root growth. Mow at least three days before applying lawn fertilizer and deliver it evenly to avoid patchy results.

REPAIR BARE PATCHES

Soil compaction, removing weeds and scalping the surface with the mower can leave unsightly bare patches. Don't worry, they're easy to repair. Remove any dead grass, loosen the soil with a fork and rake it level. Scatter grass seed at the rate specified on the manufacturer's packet, cover with a thin layer of sieved compost and sprinkle with water. It should take the seed about ten days to germinate. Protect the seed from birds by stretching plastic netting over the top.

FIX BROKEN EDGES

General wear and tear can lead to the edges of lawns breaking. Repairing is straightforward but does require a bit of elbow grease. Cut around the damaged part with a half-moon tool and undercut with a spade to remove a square of turf. Rotate it by 180 degrees, ensuring the good edge is facing outward. Chop off the flawed part of the turf piece, to leave a straight edge. Fill the gap with topsoil and sow with grass seed. Another option is to replace with a piece of fresh turf.

↓ Treat compaction by pushing a garden fork into the lawn as deeply as possible and wiggling it about to enlarge the holes. This will break through the compacted soil, while allowing air and moisture to reach the roots.

A POTTED HISTORY OF LAWNS

A passion for a verdant lawn is deeply rooted in the British national psyche. In the 18th century, lawns were a status symbol and largely restricted to landscapes created around country estates. It took an army of gardeners armed with scythes to keep them trimmed. The invention of the lawnmower in the early 19th century led to the wealthy middle classes adding patches of grass around their suburban villas. The most rapid increase in lawns took place after the First World War, when masses of houses were built on the outskirts of towns, boasting lawns in the front and back gardens.

HOW TO APPLY LAWN FERTILIZER GRANULES

It's important to spread lawn fertilizer granules evenly, otherwise you'll get patchy results or a build-up of fertilizer, which will scorch grass. Lawn fertilizer granules are easy to distribute with a wheeled spreading machine. Fill the hopper with the right amount of fertilizer for the entire lawn and set the machine to spread at half rate. Walk backward and forward in parallel lines across the length of your lawn, and repeat across the width. If you have a small lawn, scatter by hand.

MOWERS AND MOWING

By far the most important lawn care tool is a mower. A hand-push mower, hover mower or compact cordless mower is perfect for small lawns, while those with larger lawns could consider a more powerful rotary or cylinder mower. Ride-on mowers are perfect for anyone whose lawn is more extensive. Start by cutting lawns with the blades on their highest setting early in the year, reducing the height of the cut as the season progresses – an eventual height of 2.5cm (1in) is ideal for hard-wearing family lawns that mainly contain perennial ryegrass. Lawns need trimming from early spring until autumn, unless the weather is very mild over winter. As a rule of thumb, aim to cut the lawn once a week in spring and autumn, and up to twice a week in summer.

DID YOU KNOW ?

The first cylinder lawnmower rolled out of a workshop in Stroud, Gloucestershire, in 1830. Invented by engineer Edwin Beard Budding, it was a clunky heavy beast that required two men to operate. London Zoo snapped up one of the first machines – the foreman was delighted that it could carry out the work of 'eight men with scythes'.

HOW TO GET STRIPES ON YOUR LAWN

Many people consider a lawn adorned with alternating dark and light green stripes as the epitome of a formal British garden. To pull the look off, you need to use a mower fitted with a rear roller. Mow in parallel rows, with each row in the opposite direction to the next. Once the grass starts to grow, you'll lose the effect, so regular mowing is required.

> **Word buster:**
> **Crepuscular**
>
> Used to describe creatures that are active at dusk, such as bats, foxes, rabbits and moths.

↓ Start   ↓ Finish

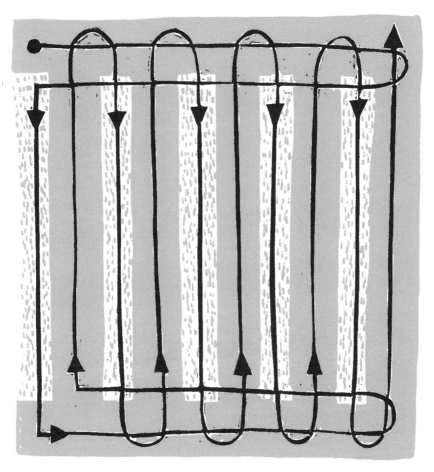

Start Sweet Peas

Sweet peas (*Lathyrus odoratus*) are nature's answer to artificial air fresheners. Sow some seeds in spring, and the long straight stems will take off, producing sprays of flowers that will infuse the summer garden with their perfume. These annual climbers like a warm, sunny and sheltered spot with fertile, well-drained soil.

FIVE GREAT SWEET PEA VARIETIES NAMED AFTER NOTABLE PEOPLE

1 'Emilia Fox'

2 'Richard and Judy'

3 'Darcey Bussell'

4 'Terry Wogan'

5 'Winston Churchill'

» HOW TO SOW & GROW FROM SEEDS «

1 Sweet pea seeds are protected by a hard shell, so soak the seeds in water overnight to soften and improve germination. Those that are plump are ideal for sowing.

2 Sow seeds 1cm (½in) deep beneath supports such as obelisks on wigwams of canes, or against walls and fences fitted with training wires. Alternatively, grow sweet peas in 45cm (18in) containers. Place a climbing structure on top and sow a seed at the base of each upright support. Shoots should appear within two to three weeks.

3 When the seedlings are about 10cm (4in) high, pinch out the growing tips to produce stronger, bushier plants.

4 As they mature, the plants will climb by twining tendrils around their supports. Give them a helping hand to start off by tying in the stems with twine.

5 Water the plants regularly, especially during warm spells. Once the flower buds appear, start feeding the plants every week with a high-potash fertilizer.

6 Ensure the plants deliver flowers all summer by picking stems regularly to display indoors and by deadheading to prevent them producing seeds.

A POTTED HISTORY OF SWEET PEAS

In 1695, a Franciscan monk named Francisco Cupani spotted an unfamiliar plant growing near his monastery in Sicily. It was the wild sweet pea, a 1.8m (6ft)-tall climber with heavily scented, bicoloured, deep purple and violet flowers. Excited about his discovery, Cupani sent seeds to botanical gardens and plant collectors around Europe. Some ended up with Robert Uvedale, a school master from Enfield, Middlesex, who in 1699 became the first person to grow sweet peas in Britain.

DID YOU KNOW ?

On 20 February 1911, the *Daily Mail* announced that it would hand out £1,000 (£120,000 at today's value) to the gardener who could grow the best sweet peas. Over 38,000 bunches were sent to the Crystal Palace exhibition centre for judging. The winner was Mrs Janet Fraser from Kelso, Scotland. Unwins Seeds later named a variety in her honour.

Make Hanging Baskets

Hanging baskets are great for breaking up the monotony of walls and fences. Mid-spring is the perfect time to plant one with summer-flowering bedding plants, allowing them to establish before they are ready for placing outdoors when there's no longer any danger from frosts - usually late spring.

For an exuberant display, go for a mixture of traditional favourites. Fuchsias, pelargoniums and heliotrope (*Heliotropium*) will provide height, while fibrous-rooted begonias, marigolds (African and French) and floss flower (*Ageratum*) are great for filling gaps. Use dichondra, helichrysum, nasturtium (*Tropaeolum*) and petunias for their trailing stems.

Special hanging basket compost is widely available but you don't need anything fancy. Peat-free potting compost fortified with a handful of controlled-release fertilizer granules and water-retaining crystals will do the job nicely.

Make planting easy by standing the basket on top of a large pot to prevent it moving. If the basket is open-sided, cover the inside with a liner and add a 2.5cm (1in) layer of compost to the base. Make slits around the outside through which trailing plants can be fed. Fill two-thirds of the container with compost and repeat the process.

If the basket has closed sides, fill it with compost until it is within a few centimetres of the rim and then plant up the top - place taller varieties at the back with more compact plants in front. Dot lower-growing specimens and trailers around the edge. Water well and stash in a light, frost-free place for the moment.

↑ Feed plants through
the outside of a hanging
basket to avoid damage
and make sure the
rootballs are well
covered with more
potting compost.

DID YOU KNOW ?

In 2009, a hanging basket measuring 6×3m (20×10ft) and weighing more than
0.25 tonnes set the record for the world's largest when it was unveiled outside
a London hotel. Set 7.5m (25ft) off the ground, the massive structure took eight
hours to hoist into position and contained 100 different plants.

Prune Frost-damaged Shrubs

Winter frosts can cause shoot tips to blacken, wither or die back, so remove damaged growth with secateurs, cutting back to healthy buds. This will encourage new shoots to grow and prevent die-back spreading down the stem. Frost damage is obvious on evergreen plants, but can be more difficult to spot on deciduous shrubs - if in any doubt, wait until the plant comes into leaf before removing any dead growth. After pruning, give plants a boost by scattering some balanced granular fertilizer granules around them, working these into the soil with a rake.

Cool Down Greenhouses

Temperatures can build up rapidly inside greenhouses on warm days, leading to plants inside starting to flag. Opening doors, vents and windows will help to keep things cool, but it's also a good idea to use a technique called 'damping down'. Simply splash staging, paths and the floor with cold water during a spell of warm weather. Do this in the morning, and over the course of the day water will evaporate and raise humidity levels, thereby reducing moisture loss from plants. As a bonus, damping down will also deter greenhouse red spider mite, a sap-sucking pest that thrives in hot dry conditions.

Improve Your Pond

Garden ponds add movement, sound and beauty to gardens, while providing a refuge for aquatic creatures and the opportunity to grow a range of plants that like wet feet. In order to keep the water clear and the plants in great shape, and to prevent the feature from becoming an eyesore, give ponds a quick spring service. Stop a sparkling pool from turning into a murky sump by twirling out blanketweed from beneath the surface with a cane or stick. Leave on the side of the pond for a day or two to allow any wildlife to return to the water, and then consign it to the compost bin. If duckweed is lying on the water surface, skim it off with a small net.

Water irises (*Iris ensata* and *I. laevigata*), Japanese rush (*Acorus gramineus*), dwarf reed mace (*Typha minima*) and many other aquatic perennials will be shy to flower if congested. Rejuvenate by carefully lifting containers from the water, removing the rootball and splitting into several smaller pieces. Repot a section into the same container using fresh aquatic compost.

Add some new plants if your pond is looking empty. Aim to cover about one-third of the surface with foliage, using a combination of floating aquatics, submerged oxygenating plants and waterlilies (*Nymphaea*), along with a vibrant selection of marginal plants grown in the shallow water around the edges of the pond.

↓The best way to remove blanketweed from under a pond's surface is by twirling it out with a cane. Don't forget to leave the blanketweed on the side of the pond for a day or two to allow aquatic creatures to return to the water.

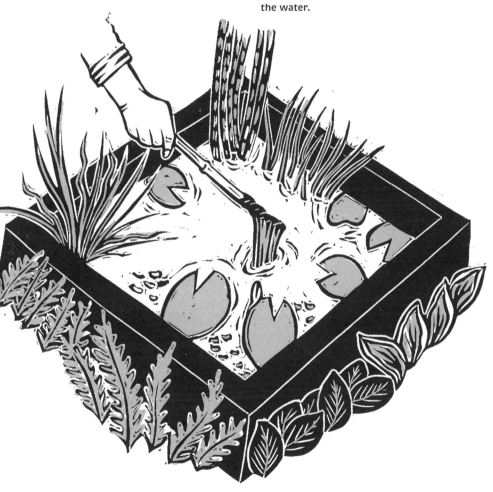

Scrumptious Strawberries

Supermarket strawberries can look and smell irresistible. However, take a bite and you'll be left with a profound sense of disappointment. Instead of being blown away by the taste and texture, it's like chewing on a wad of cotton wool that's been impregnated with a hint of strawberry flavouring.

The best way to ensure strawberries are a taste sensation is to grow your own. Those with plenty of room can set plants in beds or borders, or even start a dedicated strawberry patch. Anyone with a smaller plot can raise them in plant pots, grow-bags or hanging baskets.

TWO MAIN TYPES OF STRAWBERRY

Garden strawberries are divided into two groups based on when the berries appear. Summer-fruiting ones tend to have a single heavy flush of fruit at some point from late May to the end of August. Varieties are usually described as early, mid- or late season. The second group are known as everbearers or perpetual strawberries. These produce their first berries in June and then continue to fruit on and off lightly into autumn.

PLANTING IN THE GROUND

Strawberries prefer a sunny spot with well-drained, fertile soil. Dig in plenty of garden compost, leafmould or well-rotted manure before planting, and then space the plants 45cm (18in) apart with 1m (3ft) between rows. Scatter some general fertilizer granules around the plants to get them off to a flying start.

GROWING IN CONTAINERS

Another option is to raise strawberries in containers. A single plant is perfect in a 20cm (8in) pot filled with multipurpose potting compost, while four will provide plenty of pickings from a 40cm (16in) hanging basket. You'll also get great results from raising them in grow-bags, spacing three down each side.

HOW LONG DO STRAWBERRY PLANTS LAST?

Summer-fruiting varieties should provide you with heavy crops for around four years before they start to lose vigour. As they produce fruit over a longer period of time, everbearer strawberries tend to run out of steam far sooner. Expect to replace plants every couple of years or so.

LOOKING AFTER STRAWBERRIES

Water the plants regularly, especially during dry sunny spells, and feed every two weeks with a high-potash fertilizer once flowers appear. Avoid wetting fruits to prevent grey mould (see page 38). Strawberries are largely trouble-free, but you may need to take measures to scare off hungry birds.

HARVESTING

If you can, harvest fruit in the morning by removing the strawberry complete with its stalk, to give it a longer shelf life. To do this, pinch off the stalk with your thumb and forefinger.

END-OF-SEASON CARE

When you have picked all the strawberries, cut back tatty foliage to leave a boss of undamaged foliage at the centre of the plant. Remove or pot up the runners. In late winter, you can prune the foliage again, removing leaves that have been damaged by the weather.

FIVE GREAT STRAWBERRY VARIETIES TO TRY

1 **'Cambridge Favourite'** - a favourite of pick-your-own farms. Heavy crops are borne in June and July.

2 **'Honeoye'** - has conical-shaped, bright red berries in June and early July.

3 **'Mara des Bois'** - a French everbearer, with big aromatic berries from July until October.

4 **'Sonata'** - bears large crops of big, sweet fruit in mid-summer.

5 **'Symphony'** - is bred in Scotland and copes well with damp conditions.

A POTTED HISTORY OF STRAWBERRIES

A French spy by the name of Amédée-François Frézier is responsible for our favourite summer fruit. Sent on a mission to monitor Spanish activity in colonial Chile by King Louis XIV, he discovered fields of strawberry plants with fruit larger than the wild woodland strawberries that are native to Europe. On 17 August 1714, he docked at Marseilles with five plants. Known botanically as *Fragaria chiloensis*, this was later crossed with *F. virginiana*, a North American species, resulting in *F. × ananassa*, which is the parent of most modern varieties.

DID YOU KNOW ?

Around two million strawberries are served annually at the Wimbledon tennis championships. 'Elsanta', 'Malling Centenary' and 'Sonata' are among the main varieties harvested for the event, while 'Jubilee' is served in the royal box.

How to Grow Rhubarb

The tart stems of rhubarb are delicious in a host of savoury dishes or, tempered with sweetener, in classic dessert ones. Pot-grown plants are available all year round, while bare-root crowns are sold from late autumn until mid-spring. Raise rhubarb in a sunny open spot with moist, free-draining soil and work in plenty of well-rotted manure.

PLANTING CROWNS

Plant crowns in holes that are the same depth as the woody rhizome and just a little wider. Set them in the centre, spread out the roots and plant so the tip bearing shoots is just visible above the surface of the soil. Use your fingers to firm the soil around the roots to remove any air pockets.

HARVESTING

Avoid picking stems during the year the rhubarb plant was planted in order to allow it to use all of its energy for building up a strong root system. Feel free to sample a few stems the following spring and summer but don't go mad. From then on, you can pick up to half of the stems, leaving some intact to ensure the plant remains in active growth.

LOOKING AFTER PLANTS

Keep rhubarb plants in good shape by mulching in spring and feeding with a balanced general fertilizer. Water regularly during summer, and remove any flower stalks that appear. Clear up the foliage when it dies back in autumn, to expose the crown to frost - this will help to break dormancy and encourage good crops.

A POTTED HISTORY OF RHUBARB

Nobody knows where rhubarb originates but the ancient Chinese were cultivating plants for medicinal use as far back as 2700BC. It was highly prized by merchants and exported along the Silk Road, reaching Europe in the 14th century. The first record of rhubarb being eaten in Britain was in the late 1700s. At the time, it was considered a medicinal plant, and it wasn't until the wide availability of sugar in the 18th century that it became a culinary treat.

FIVE GREAT RHUBARB VARIETIES TO TRY

1 **'Champagne'** - an old variety with slender, pale pink stalks.

2 **'Fulton's Strawberry Surprise'** - an attractive variety with vivid red stems.

3 **'Stockbridge Arrow'** - bred in Yorkshire, this variety has distinctive, arrow-shaped leaves.

4 **'Timperley Early'** - a heritage variety with two-tone pink and green stems.

5 **'Victoria'** - named in honour of Queen Victoria after her coronation in 1837.

FORCED RHUBARB

Rhubarb plants naturally produce stems that can be harvested between April and early June, but professional growers have developed a method of producing out-of-season stalks. Dormant crowns are lifted from fields in November and packed into heated windowless buildings lit by candles. Energy stored in the roots encourages plants to grow but lack of sunlight prevents photosynthesis, resulting in pale tender sticks that are available from early winter until mid-spring. Remarkably, forced rhubarb was discovered by accident in 1817, when gardeners at the Chelsea Physic Garden covered a dormant plant with soil. Several weeks later, they removed the soil and found shoots had developed underneath.

To produce your own forced rhubarb, pack straw over dormant plants in winter and then cover with a traditional terra-cotta forcing jar, bucket or an upturned pot, making sure that you block out all light. Keep the cover in place for at least six weeks before having a peak. The stems are ready for harvesting when they are about 23cm (9in) long. Avoid picking any stems for the next two years to allow the plant to recover.

RHUBARB: FRUIT OR VEG?

It's an age-old gardening conundrum...is rhubarb a fruit or a vegetable? Well, this question was at the heart of a legal battle in 1947, when a US customs court ruled that rhubarb was a fruit. As a result, exports from across the border in Canada were subject to higher tariffs than if it had been classified as a vegetable. It later emerged that the judgment was an act of protectionism aimed at giving American rhubarb growers an advantage, and it was overturned. In fact, rhubarb is technically a vegetable that's eaten as a dessert once the tart stems have been sweetened.

Support Perennials

Nothing compares to a bed or border in summer, but a display can turn into an unsightly mess unless you support some perennials. Take measures now to shore up top-heavy, weak-stemmed or naturally floppy perennials, so they're less likely to be blown over, flattened by rain or else collapse under the weight of their own flowers.

WHEN TO STAKE PLANTS

It's best to add plant supports before perennials have put on too much growth, usually when they are 15cm (6in) or so in height. Shoots will grow through supports and hide these, resulting in a natural-looking display. If left until later, it can be difficult to put the supports in place without damaging the plants, and they will also be visible.

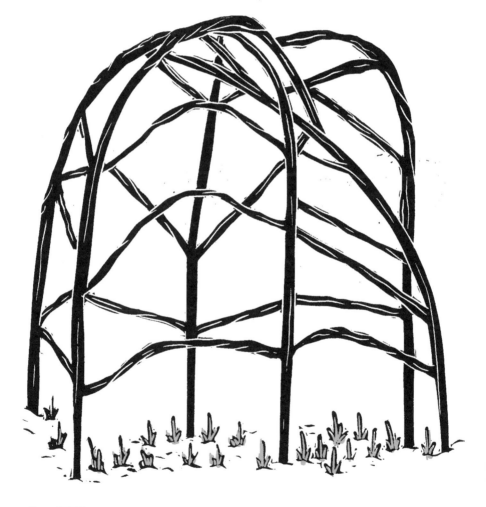

- Peasticks are handy for bolstering clumps of multistemmed perennials such as cranesbill (*Geranium*), herbaceous clematis and Oriental poppies (*Papaver orientale*). Traditionally, lengths of hazel (*Corylus*) and willow (*Salix*) were used, but any twiggy branches will do. Position the peasticks around the perimeter, angle them slightly inward and weave the tops together to make a dome shape, 15cm (6in) lower than the eventual height of the plant.

- Linking stakes connect together to allow sizeable clumps of weak-stemmed perennials - yarrow (*Achillea*), gypsophila, bellflower (*Campanula*) and the like - to be completely encircled. Push the stakes into the soil to one-half the plant's eventual height. Shorter stakes are ideal at the front of borders to prevent lax-stemmed plants flopping onto a lawn or path.

- Use grow-through ring supports to support weak-stemmed perennials with large flowerheads or those that tend to flop before flowering. Push the support into the ground above each individual clump and pull up slightly as the plant grows, stopping once it's at one-half the mature height of the plant. Use for Peruvian lilies (*Alstroemeria*), sedums (*Hylotelephium*) and coneflowers (*Rudbeckia*).

- Single-stem loop supports are perfect for taller perennials such as delphiniums and foxtail lilies (*Eremurus*). There are two main types: a solid forged stake with an open loop at the top and a steel rod with an adjustable ring. Choose one that will support up to one-half of the mature height of the stem with a loop wide enough to accommodate it comfortably.

'If you have a garden and a library, you have everything you need.'

Marcus Tullius Cicero

How to Grow Carrots

Most dictionaries describe carrots along these lines... 'a tapering, orange-coloured root'. In fact, they are much more diverse than this. Carrots can be round, stumpy, conical, slender or candle-shaped, measuring 2.5-30cm (1-12in) in length. Apart from orange ones, there are also white, yellow, red and purple varieties.

TWO MAIN TYPES OF CARROT

There are two main types: early and maincrop. Early ones are ideal for sowing between spring and early summer, and are ready for harvesting seven weeks later. Sow maincrop varieties from April onward; they should be ready to lift in 11 weeks, but are tough enough to survive in the ground over winter.

SOWING SEEDS

Carrots prefer light, stone-free soil and a sunny spot. Prepare the soil by digging, removing weeds and large stones, and then rake until the texture resembles coarse breadcrumbs. Make a shallow trench, 1cm (½in) deep, with the corner of a rake and sow seed thinly along the base. When they've germinated, nip off the leaves of weaker seedlings to leave plants 25cm (10in) apart. Allow a gap of 30cm (12in) between rows.

A POTTED HISTORY OF CARROTS

Carrots are believed to have originated from an area that is now part of modern-day Iran and Afghanistan. Wild plants had spindly purple or black roots with a bitter taste, and it wasn't until seeds were transported by merchants to Europe, Africa and Asia that larger, tastier and more productive roots appeared. Early cultivated carrots were red, yellow, white and purple in colour – the first orange carrots were developed in Holland in the 16th century.

DID YOU KNOW ?

Rationing during the Second World War meant that many foodstuffs were in short supply, but carrots were readily available. As a result, the Ministry of Food launched a campaign led by a cartoon character known as Doctor Carrot, who urged the nation to eat more orange roots. Described as 'the children's best friend', he was featured carrying a bag marked Vit. A.

RAISING CARROTS IN POTS

If you are strapped for space, try growing carrots in 20cm (8in) pots filled with soil-based potting compost, such as John Innes No 2. Sow seed in rows or scatter thinly over the surface and cover with a 1cm (½in) layer of compost. When the seedlings appear, thin to about 10cm (4in) apart.

FIVE GREAT CARROT VARIETIES TO TRY

1 **'Amsterdam Forcing 3'** - small, blunt-ended roots with a sweet taste.

2 **'Chantenay Red Cored 3 - Supreme'** - sweet-tasting, 10cm (4in)-long, stumpy carrots.

3 **'Early Nantes'** - a French variety with long cylindrical roots.

4 **'Jaune du Doubs'** - a yellow-skinned variety bred in France.

5 **'Purple Haze'** - a dark purple carrot with an orange core.

BEAT CARROT FLY

Carrots are generally trouble-free, but can be bothered by carrot fly. The pest is attracted by the smell of roots after seedlings have been thinned out. It then lays its eggs, which hatch into burrowing larvae. To avoid problems, sow carrots thinly, to reduce the need for editing - if you do need to thin out, pinch the foliage off to avoid disturbing the roots. As a further precaution, cover crops with some fine mesh to prevent adult flies reaching them.

MAKE A TRADITIONAL STORAGE CLAMP

A glut of carrots at an allotment can be stored in an insulated outdoor structure known as a clamp. To make a simple clamp, place a sheet of polythene on the ground and cover it with a layer of straw. Arrange a layer of carrots in a circular pattern, covering with more straw. Continue to build up the layers, making a cone-shaped structure. Once finished, spread straw over the structure and then cover with a 15cm (6in) layer of soil.

FACT OR FICTION?

Many children have grown up being told to eat up their carrots as they help you to see in the dark. But is this actually true? Carrots contain vitamin A, required by our eyes to produce a pigment that allows them to work in low light levels. Vitamin A deficiency hinders vision but eating more carrots doesn't make them work better than normal. The myth was started by the British government during the Second World War. In an attempt to keep the Royal Air Force's use of radar secret from the German high command, they spread the rumour that fighter pilots were able to shoot down enemy bombers at night because they were eating lots of carrots to help them see in the dark. It's not known whether the Germans were fooled, but the average Brit certainly thought there was some truth in it. The story was given credibility by the Ministry of Food, which issued posters claiming that eating carrots would 'help you to see in the blackout'.

Grow Chives

A perennial herb, chives (*Allium schoenoprasum*) are grown for their pungent leaves with a mild onion taste. These are delicious when chopped up finely and mixed into a salad or added to hot dishes - they work particularly well with potatoes, eggs and soft cheese. Even their pretty pink flowers are edible and make an attractive garnish.

Mature chive plants are readily available, but they are super easy to start from seed. Sow a few seeds thinly in a small pot and place in a heated propagator. When the seedlings are large enough, divide the rootball into several pieces. Plant in groups of three, spaced about 20cm (8in) apart, or in pots filled with soil-based potting compost.

Chives thrive in moisture-retentive, well-drained soil in a sunny or partially shaded spot. Keep plants well-watered during dry spells in summer, and ensure they remain productive by removing flowers as they fade. Cut leaves as required with scissors, snipping close to the base of plants.

WHAT TO GROW

○ **Bog-standard, common chives** (*A. schoenoprasum*) - the one you're most likely to find for sale in garden centres. For named varieties check out the offerings of mail-order seed companies.

○ *Allium schoenoprasum* **'Fine-leaved'** - has a milder flavour than common chives and also thinner leaves.

○ *Allium schoenoprasum* **'Black Isle Blush'** - boasts showier, light mauve flowers with deep pink centres.

○ *Allium schoenoprasum* **'Forescate'** - has slightly garlic-flavoured leaves and pale pink flowers.

TOP TIP

Chives are best used fresh, although they can be cut up finely, packed into an ice-cube tray half-filled with water and popped into the freezer. Whenever you need some chives for a recipe, simply knock out as many ice cubes as you need and add to the pan.

DID YOU KNOW ?

Chives have been eaten in China for thousands of years, and Venetian explorer and traveller Marco Polo is credited with publicizing their culinary benefits throughout Europe in the late 13th century.

Start Peas from Seed

Home-grown peas are so much better than any 'fresh' peas sold in supermarkets. It doesn't matter whether it is bags of pods or packs of hand-shelled peas, within minutes of being harvested the natural sugars inside the flesh start to convert to starch and their flavour and texture are impaired. Those with a large veg plot and a big appetite for peas might like to sow a few seeds every couple of weeks until the end of July, which will provide pickings well into November.

TWO TYPES OF PEA

Technically, there are two main types of pea. 'Round' ones are perfect for sowing in autumn and picking the following spring, while 'wrinkled' peas are best for sowing in summer, as they have craggy skin that traps water and can lead to rotting in cold soil over winter.

HOW TO GROW SEEDS

Make a shallow trench, 23cm (9in) wide and 2.5cm (1in) deep. An easy way to create a furrow is to pull soil back with a draw hoe. Sow seeds in two parallel lines, spacing them 5cm (2in) apart. Cover with soil excavated from the trench and water. Space subsequent rows about 90cm (36in) apart to provide access for maintenance.

→To experience the taste sensation of really fresh peas, sow seed in a sunny spot and you'll be picking handfuls of pods by the end of summer.

IN THE GUTTER

Mice foraging for seeds can be a problem on some allotments. A clever way to thwart them is to start peas indoors using a piece of plastic guttering. Drill some drainage holes, fill with potting compost and pop in the pea seeds. When the seedlings are 10cm (4in) tall, dig a narrow trench outdoors and slide the contents of the guttering into position.

SUPPORTING PLANTS

When seedlings are 5cm (2in) tall, add some supports to prevent them collapsing under their own weight. A few twiggy sticks set into the ground at regular intervals will do for compact varieties. Taller ones will need something more substantial, such as a sheet of support netting attached to a row of 1.8m (6ft)-tall bamboo canes.

LOOKING AFTER THEM

Remove any weeds that appear, so they do not compete for moisture and nutrients, and water plants regularly, especially during warm dry spells. Apart from ensuring the pea pods swell, watering prevents problems with downy mildew disease, which tends to be worst when the soil is dry.

HARVESTING

Peas will generally be ready for picking about three months after sowing. Ensure a steady supply by picking regularly to encourage more pods to develop - those at the bottom will generally be the first to mature. To avoid damaging plants, cut pods off individually with scissors and don't attempt to pull them off by hand.

FOUR GREAT PEA VARIETIES TO TRY

1 **'Hurst Green Shaft'** - bred in Lincolnshire back in the late 1960s, this variety grows to 75cm (2½ft) in height and has heavy crops of well-filled pods of wrinkled peas.

2 **'Kelvedon Wonder'** - making its debut in the 1930s in Essex, this heavy-yielding variety produces pods packed with up to eight succulent round peas.

3 **'Rondo'** - renowned for its taste and high yields, this produces straight pods up to 10cm (4in) in length with an average of ten wrinkled peas.

4 **'Terrain'** - highly resistant to both downy and powdery mildew, this wrinkled variety produces curved pods containing up to eight peas.

MYSTERY OF THE MUMMY PEAS

Egyptomania swept across Europe during the 19th and early 20th centuries, largely as a result of Napoleon Bonaparte's campaign in Egypt and the discovery of ancient monuments. Pea seeds were often found in tombs explored by archaeologists and became a popular souvenir for those visiting Egypt during this period. So-called mummy or Egyptian peas were often advertised for sale with one advertisement. claiming 'the growth of this pea is different to those in this country' and 'the taste is unequalled'. Alas, it was all an elaborate ruse. In 2002, botanists at Kew concluded that it would be impossible for seeds to remain viable after 3,000 years.

PROJECT: How to Restore Secateurs

A pair of good-quality secateurs is an essential cutting tool. Keep them in good working order by giving them an overhaul, making sure the working parts move smoothly and the blades are sharp - blunt edges can tear or damage stems, leading to rotting or infection.

YOU WILL NEED

- Secateurs ∘ Soapy water ∘ Scrubbing brush
- Empty jar ∘ White vinegar ∘ Cloth
- Sharpening stone or secateurs sharpening file ∘ Thin oil

HOW TO DO IT

1 Take your secateurs apart, including any removable springs and blades. Use soapy water to scrub off any encrusted dirt from the handles.

2 Submerge the blade in a jar of white vinegar and leave overnight to soak. In the morning, rub with a cloth. Acetic acid in the vinegar will remove rust and dried-on sap.

3 Sharpen the blade with a sharpening stone or a secateurs sharpening file. Hone the cutting edge first, following the angle of the blade.

4 Lubricate the springs and other moving parts with thin oil. Finish by putting the pieces back together again.

Pest and Disease Watch: Box Tree Moth

Accidently introduced from Asia, box tree moth was first recorded in southeast England in 2007 and is now widespread around the UK. Flying between late July and mid-September, the moth lays its eggs on box (*Buxus*) plants, and these hatch into ravenous, black-headed caterpillars that eat leaves and even bark. The pest is a big problem for box hedge owners, causing patches of dead growth. Check for caterpillars, their webbing and droppings. If present, pick off by hand. Treat infestations with an organic insecticide.

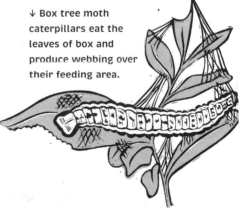

↓ Box tree moth caterpillars eat the leaves of box and produce webbing over their feeding area.

'Will you go a-maying, a-maying, a-maying,

Come and be my Queen of May and pluck the may with me?'

(E Nesbit, *May Day*)

THE MONTH AT A GLANCE

- Remove frost protection from exotics to prevent it hampering new growth.
- Protect auricula primroses from rain (see The Traditional Way to Display Auricula Primroses, page 98).
- Snip off old or tatty leaves from lungwort (*Pulmonaria*), to encourage fresh foliage.
- Remove green shoots from variegated plants (see Deal with Reversion, page 94).
- Cut the flowering stems of stinking hellebore (*Helleborus foetidus*) and *H. argutifolius* to ground level (see Trim Hellebores, page 11).
- Give plants the Chelsea chop (page 98).
- Deadhead rhododendrons (see page 98).
- Remove fading flowers from tulips.
- Deadhead lilac (*Syringa*) flowers.
- Remove the central flower spike from a clump of rhubarb.
- Thin out vegetable seedlings before they become too crowded.
- Create seedbeds for growing edibles (see Create a Seedbed, page 97).
- Sow French bean seeds (see How to Grow French Beans, page 104).
- Buy and sow seeds of pumpkins and winter squash (see How to Grow Pumpkins & Winter squash, page 106).
- Sow sweetcorn seeds in blocks outside (see How to Grow Sweetcorn, page 108).
- Plant waterlilies (*Nymphaea*) in ponds (see Improve Your Pond, page 98).
- Start a square foot gardening bed (see What is Square Foot Gardening?, page 96).
- Splash water across greenhouse floors and benches on warm days to help raise humidity (see Cool Down Greenhouses, page 78).
- Cover greenhouses with white shade paint or install internal shade netting (see Keep Greenhouses Cool, page 142).
- Remove slippery algae and dirt from hard surfaces with a pressure washer (see Clean Hard Surfaces, page 97).

May

In late spring, all of the tender edibles and ornamentals
raised from seeds or plugs earlier in the season are
ready to go outdoors as frosts are rare in many parts
of the country. It's quite liberating to reclaim your
windowsills and greenhouse benches from young
plants, and also satisfying to see something you've
raised from scratch take its place in your garden. The
weather is often warm and pleasant in May, and plants
respond positively to the heat and longer days by
seemingly growing before your very eyes.

Start Hardening Off

If you have raised plants from seed indoors, whether ornamental or edible, the seedlings will need a period of 'hardening off' before being planted in the ground or in pots. It may sound like a complicated procedure but it's nothing to worry about - it simply means acclimatizing the cossetted seedlings from indoors to a new life outdoors. The reason for this is that cooler temperatures, wind and higher light levels can check a plant's growth, so it's best to introduce seedlings to the garden gradually. Two weeks before you intend planting out, move the seedlings outside during the day (place them in a sheltered, partially shaded spot) and move them back indoors at night. Do this for a week and then place them outside 24/7, covering with fleece - for the last three days, remove the material during the day. After this, the seedlings should be tough enough to cope with garden life.

Deal with Reversion

A problem with some variegated plants is that they are prone to reversion, a growth disorder that results in the appearance of pure green shoots. Apart from looking unsightly, these sprigs are more vigorous than variegated ones and will eventually take over the plant. To prevent this from happening, snip off any all-green shoots at the main stem or base of the plant. Among the plants most likely to be affected are holly (*Ilex*), euonymus, elaeagnus, privet (*Ligustrum*) and *Acer negundo* 'Flamingo'.

Tips for Designing a Border

A well-designed border is one of the most desirable of all garden features. Most are planted to reach their peak in summer, but with careful selection of plants it's possible for these displays to add interest all year round.

SIZE AND SHAPE

Straight-edged borders that follow the boundary wall or fence are suitable for formal spaces, but those with a curved outline are more visually interesting. Narrow borders might be necessary if space is tight but, if you can, provide a depth of around 1.5m (5ft).

PREPARE THE GROUND

Mark out the outline of geometric borders with string attached to pegs. Strip back the turf, then dig over the soil and rake it level. Define the outline of curved borders by laying hosepipe along the ground and bending it to the desired shape.

GIVE PLANTING A THEME

A random selection of plants will look chaotic, so pick plants that suit a theme, such as Mediterranean or cottage garden. Alternatively, choose a colour scheme, like a hot border of reds, oranges and yellows, or perhaps a cooler one of greens and whites.

CREATE A TIERED DISPLAY

As a rule, it's best to arrange plants in borders according to their height, to establish a layered planting that graduates in height. Place lofty specimens at the back and shorter plants with floppy growth at the front. Everything else can be planted in between these two layers.

PLANTING IN ODD NUMBERS

If you want borders that are easy on the eye, avoid dotting them with lots of individual plants. It's best to arrange plants in groups of three, five, seven and so on. Pop in a few lone taller specimens to provide some interesting structure and act as focal points.

PLACE YOUR PLANTS

Arrange the plants on the ground while they are still in their pots. Tinker with the arrangement, if necessary. Once happy, decant them from their pots and plant. The distance required between plants will vary depending on their mature size. Don't worry if the planting looks gappy, because the plants will soon spread.

How to Care for Plug Plants

Plug plants are essentially well-rooted seedlings that are supplied by mail-order nurseries in spring. They are a great option for those who don't want to raise plants from seeds or are pressed for time. To ensure they thrive, water immediately upon arrival if the compost seems dry - stand the plants in a saucer of water and let them soak it up from the base. When the compost is visibly damp, place the plants on a dry saucer to allow excess water to drain. Pot the plug plants up into 7.5-9cm (3-3½in) pots of peat-free, multipurpose potting compost. Water gently with a can fitted with a sprinkler head and stand the plants in a light place indoors but out of hot direct sunlight. To avoid a check to growth, move the plants into slightly larger pots once you notice their roots are starting to poke through the drainage holes at the base. Before planting outdoors, toughen them up by hardening off (see page 94).

Effective Watering

One of the main causes of plants dying is poor watering technique. For example, lightly sprinkling the ground encourages shallow rooting, making plants susceptible to drought. However, drenching the soil beneath plants promotes longer roots that are able to find moisture deeper underground.

Ideally, water plants in the cool of the morning or evening. This gives them plenty of time to soak up moisture, rather than it evaporating quickly in warm sunshine. Watering at these times also allows droplets that land on leaves time to dry out, so avoiding scorch damage caused by strong sunlight.

A good option for keeping containers sated is to set up an automatic irrigation system, which delivers water from tiny sprinklers at specific times via a computerized timer or smartphone app. Porous hose is perfect for snaking around plants in beds and borders.

WHAT IS SQUARE FOOT GARDENING?

Square foot gardening is a space-saving way of growing vegetables which originates from the USA. The system works by dividing a 90 × 90cm (3 × 3ft) raised bed into nine 30 × 30cm (1 × 1ft) squares then hammering nails around the edge and running strings across to make a grid pattern. The raised bed can be placed on a patio, lawn or soil, and is ideal for compact crops such as peppers and beetroot.

Create a Seedbed

In order for vegetable seeds to germinate and grow, it's important to cultivate the soil by creating a seedbed. Remove any weeds or surface vegetation, and then loosely fork over the ground, breaking up large clods with the back of the fork. Rake the soil vigorously in one direction, and then work in another direction, 90 degrees to the first. Make sure you draw the soil into hollow, and level out any mounds. The soil is ready for sowing once the surface is level and the top 5-7.5cm (2-3in) has the texture of coarse breadcrumbs.

Successional Sowing

To ensure you get the most out of a veg patch during the growing season, consider successional sowing. This means sowing or planting a specific crop at regular intervals to ensure you have a constant supply of fresh produce, rather than just one glut. This technique is ideal for a wide range of edibles such as beetroot, carrot, lettuce, mixed salad leaves, radish and spring onions. Ideally, sow your next lot of seeds at around the same time as the leaves of the first batch nose their way above the soil.

Clean Hard Surfaces

Make the most of dry bright days by cleaning patios, paths, decks and driveways. Over the past few months, a combination of moss, algae and dirt from traipsing feet will have taken its toll, leaving outdoor surfaces looking terribly grimy and slippery to walk on, when wet. The quickest way of shifting dirt is to use a pressure washer on a high setting, which will leave surfaces sparkling for the rest of the season. If you don't have such a washer, use soapy water and a broom with stiff bristles to scrub the area. White vinegar is useful for getting rid of stubborn stains.

Trivia time

In 1607, James I (James VI of Scotland) asked the nobility of Britain to plant 10,000 white mulberry (*Morus alba*) trees in order to help start a home-spun silk industry. The leaves of the white mulberry are an important part of the diet of silkworms, but someone messed up the order and black mulberry (*M. nigra*) trees were delivered instead. Unfortunately, silkworms don't like these as much, and the silk industry fizzled out before it had even started.

Give Plants the Chelsea Chop

One way to avoid staking some perennials is to do the 'Chelsea chop', a cutting technique that has long been used by nursery owners to revive plants exhibited at the RHS Chelsea Flower Show. In late May, prune lanky stems back by about one-half; plants will respond with a flush of sturdy growth that is less likely to flop. As a result of such pruning, flowering will be delayed for up to six weeks. Among plants that respond well to this treatment are sedum (*Hylotelephium*), coneflowers (*Rudbeckia* and *Echinacea*), helenium and golden rod (*Solidago*).

The Traditional Way to Display Auricula Primroses

Auriculas are the aristocrats of the primrose world, with short stalks holding clusters of fragrant, single or double flowers in a wide array of shades and colour combinations. They are hybrids developed between *Primula auricula* and *P. hirsuta*.

The traditional way of displaying auriculas in pots is to place them inside an auricula theatre, which is a structure containing tiers of shelves with a roof to protect the plants from wind, rain and strong sunshine. Historians believe these were first used back in the 1600s. The oldest remaining structure in Britain can be found at Calke Abbey in Derbyshire. Built in the 1830s, it consists of a wooden frame, 5.7m (19ft) long and 2.7m (9ft) high, set around a 1.2m (4ft)-deep brick recess covered by a sloping roof. Inside, there's room for 200 auriculas on a bank of eight shelves.

Deadhead Rhododendrons

For tidy-looking rhododendrons and a great display of flowers next spring, deadhead the flowers as they fade. Nipping off the blooms ensures the plant produces new flower-bearing shoots, rather than putting its energy into seed production. Use your thumb and forefinger to snap the heads off, just above a set of leaves.

Name explain: Fuschia

Fuchsias are named after Leonhart Fuchs, a trailblazing, 16th-century German botanist. Sadly, he never saw the plants that commemorate his name as he died 130 years before a wild species was discovered by French plant hunter Charles Plumier, on the Caribbean island of Hispaniola in 1696

Lovely Lilacs

Lilacs (*Syringa*) are admired for their dense conical flowerheads that appear in late spring and early summer. Carrying a strong sweet perfume that can be detected from a great distance, the blooms come in shades of white, yellow, pink, near red, lilac, blue and purple. Plants range in height from around 1.5m (6ft) to whoppers above 6m (20ft), with a spread to match. Lilacs like a sunny spot and prefer well-drained, neutral soil but are so easy-going that they'll tolerate chalky or even slightly acidic conditions.

Plant lilacs as specimens in lawns or use them to add structure to beds and borders. They also make a delightful flowering hedge if you set individual plants 50cm (20in) apart in a row. Compact ones are great subjects for patio containers. Plant them in 45cm (18in)-diameter pots, using a 50:50 mixture of peat-free, multipurpose potting compost and John Innes No 3. Larger species will be fine in containers for a couple of years or so, but are so vigorous that they'll sulk if their roots are confined for any longer than that.

Once the flowers start to fade, wait until you can clearly see two shoots starting to swell on stems directly underneath and then deadhead. Lilacs look best as open-centred, multistemmed shrubs with about ten stems. Remove one or two stems each winter, to encourage plants to produce new stems from the base.

THREE LOVELY LILAC VARIETIES TO TRY

1 *S. meyeri* 'Palibin' - a slow-growing shrub eventually reaching 1.5m (5ft) in height with upright spikes of fragrant, lilac-pink flowers.

2 *S. vulgaris* 'Charles Joly' - introduced by Victor Lemoine in 1896, this boasts clusters of fragrant, double, dark purple flowers.

3 *S. vulgaris* 'Sensation' - launched in 1938, this variety produces large, heavily scented panicles of white-edged, purple flowers.

A POTTED HISTORY OF LILACS

Lilacs are a tribe of deciduous shrubs that are native to a huge tract of land, from southeast Europe to east Asia, where they are found in woodland. Their botanical name *Syringa* comes from the Greek word *syrinx*, meaning 'hollow tube' - in ancient Greece, pith was drilled out of their stems to make flutes and panpipes. Lilacs didn't really become popular garden plants until the late 1800s, when French nurseryman Victor Lemoine introduced a raft of highly scented varieties of *S. vulgaris*, a species that comes from the Balkan Peninsula. After Lemoine's death in 1911, his family nursery continued to breed new lilacs until 1968. During its tenure, an estimated 214 different lilacs rolled off the nursery production line.

Make a Splash with Waterlilies

Waterlilies (*Nymphaea*) are the undisputed summer-flowering stars of the aquatic world, capable of providing a touch of glamour to any body of water. Often flowering from June until September, they are ideal for planting anytime between March and October.

There are varieties suitable for just about every water feature, from a 15cm (6in)-deep container pond to a 1.8m (6ft)-deep lake. Plants will produce a succession of pads on long stalks, enabling them to spread anywhere from 20cm (8in) to more than 2.4m (8ft).

The often-scented, cup- or star-shaped blooms of waterliles come in shades of white, yellow, pink, red and blue-purple, and they range in size from 2.5cm (1in) to 40cm (16in) across. The single, semidouble or double flowers last anywhere from three to five days before they wither.

Waterlilies are usually sold in mesh-sided pots that allows gases to escape and the free movement of water. Prior to popping in the pond, spread a thick layer of washed grit over the surface to prevent compost from being stirred up by moving water or fish. Then lower each container slowly into the pond, allowing air bubbles to rise as the compost fills with water. Don't sink it in too quickly or else the grit will be washed off the top. If you can't reach the bottom of the container easily, thread some lengths of twine through each corner and submerge into position.

Trivia time

The world's largest waterlily is *Victoria amazonica*, a species from tropical South America. The leaves measure up to 3m (10ft) across and are carried on stalks up to 8m (26ft) in length.

DID YOU KNOW ?

A display of waterlilies staged by nurseryman Joseph Bory Latour-Marliac at the 1899 World Fair in Paris caught the eye of Impressionist artist Claude Monet. Five years later, Monet placed an order for some waterlilies with Latour-Marliac to grow in his pond at Giverny. These plants were the main focus of his artistic attention during the last 22 years of his life, appearing in nearly 250 paintings.

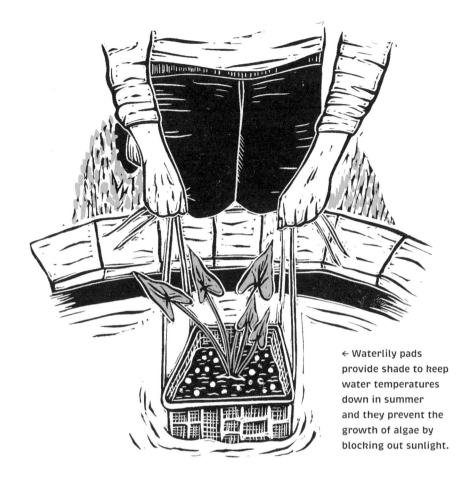

← Waterlily pads provide shade to keep water temperatures down in summer and they prevent the growth of algae by blocking out sunlight.

FIVE WONDERFUL WATERLILIES TO TRY

1 'Aurora' - dating from 1895, this cracking dwarf variety has yellow cup-shaped flowers that change colour as they mature, deepening to orange and then red.

2 'Graziella' a compact type that's ideal for container ponds, with 13cm (5in)-wide pads and tiny, apricot-pink flowers.

3 'Perry's Baby Red' - a dwarf variety from 1983 that's perfect in container ponds, forming a mat of tiny pads with 5cm (2in)-wide flowers.

4 'Perry's Double White' - perfect in water 60-75cm (24-30in) deep, this variety boasts striking, white, double flowers, which are sweetly scented.

5 'Pygmaea Helvola' - a super-compact form with flowers the size of a 50p piece and 12cm (5in)-wide, green leaves mottled with red.

PROJECT: Make a Simple Raised Bed

Raised bed kits are widely available but it's easy for those with the most basic DIY skills to knock a raised bed together in next to no time. A 130 × 70cm (51 × 28in), two-tier bed is suitable for most gardens and should take only a few hours to build.

YOU WILL NEED

- 4 × 130cm (51in)-long planks of 225 × 50mm (9 × 2in) pressure-treated timber for the sides
- 4 × 70cm (28in)-long planks of 225 × 50mm (9 × 2in) pressure-treated timber for the ends
- 4 × 45cm (18in)-long pieces of 50 × 50mm (2 × 2in) pressure-treated timber for the corner stakes
- Wood saw ◦ Exterior screws and screwdriver ◦ Engineer's square
- Drill and wood drill bit ◦ Waterproof sheeting ◦ Sterilized top soil
- Peat-free, multipurpose potting compost ◦ Horticultural grit
- Controlled-release fertilizer granules

HOW TO DO IT

1 Prepare the site by clearing away existing vegetation.

2 Screw the planks to the corner stakes to create a rectangular bed using the engineer's square to ensure the shape isn't wonky. Once the first tier is completed, continue with the next level.

3 Line the inside with waterproof sheeting.

4 Fill the raised bed with a 50:50 mix of sterilized topsoil and peat-free, multipurpose potting compost, to which horticultural grit and controlled-release fertilizer granules have been added.

The Benefits of Raised Beds

A raised bed is a square or rectangular frame that's filled with a mixture of compost and soil, and is used for growing ornamentals or vegetables. It can be made from timber, stone, brick, metal, plastic or other materials. Here are five reasons to add a raised bed to your garden.

° Some gardens have poor soil in which it is difficult to grow plants. Raised beds can be filled with moisture-retentive, free-draining soil in which most plants will thrive.

° Depending on the materials used, raised beds can be attractive features in their own right, adding height, structure and shape to a garden.

° Raised beds are perfect for filling with specialist growing media to provide conditions for plants that require specific soil, such as acid lovers.

° Their height makes raised beds a useful way to garden if you have a bad back or restricted mobility that prevents easy bending.

° Raised beds are easy to maintain. There is less space to weed compared to traditional beds, and the soil requires less upkeep as it won't become compacted under foot.

↓When building a series of raised beds in large gardens or allotments, leave a gap of at least 45cm (18in) between structures to allow for wheelbarrow access.

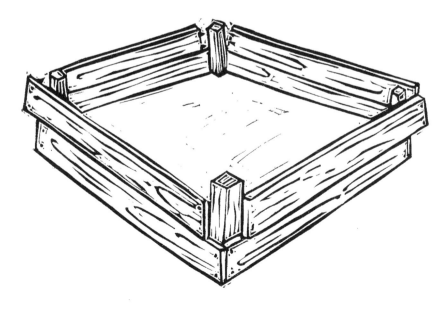

How to Grow French Beans

French bean is an umbrella name for a host of different beans, including haricot vert, fine, string, cannellini, flageolet, kidney and borlotti bean. Most are grown for their young pods, but some types are allowed to remain on plants until mature, and are then shelled for the seeds inside, which can be stored away for winter use.

Climbing varieties need something to clamber up. Construct a traditional A-frame (see page 128) or else create a wigwam of canes by spacing out five or more canes in a circular pattern, about 90cm (36in) in diameter. Make sure they're pushed firmly into the ground, then lash the tops together with twine.

Plant seeds directly into the soil any time from late May until early July. Make a 5cm (2in) hole at the foot of each cane, drop in two seeds, fill with soil and water. If both seeds germinate, remove the weakest. The plants will cling to the supports by themselves eventually, but you should help young ones on their way by securing each gently to a cane, with twine.

Dwarf French beans are sown in exactly the same way as climbing types, but there's no need to put any supports in place as plants grow only to around knee height. However, if your garden is exposed to strong winds, it helps to plant them 15cm (6in) apart in blocks, so they're propped up by their neighbours.

Water sparingly until the plants are established, increasing the amount you give them after the first flowers appear and until the last of the pods have been picked. Most beans will be ready to harvest about eight weeks after sowing. Those that are small, young and tender taste best - if you leave them for too long, they'll become tough and lose their flavour.

FIVE GREAT FRENCH BEAN VARIETIES TO TRY

1 **'Blauhilde'** - bears large bunches of 27cm (11in)-long, purple pods on 1.8m (6ft)-tall stems.

2 **'Lamon'** - a climbing borlotti bean with red-streaked pods containing fat meaty seeds with speckled skin.

3 **'Purple Teepee'** - produces cylindrical purple pods on bushy plants 45cm (18in) tall.

4 **'Yin Yang'** - a dwarf kidney type with pods crammed with a number of black-and-white patterned beans that are ideal for drying.

5 **'Impero Bianco'** - dwarf, bushy plants up to 45cm (18in) in height carry creamy yellow pods that protect up to seven white cannellini beans.

→ A traditional 'A-frame' support takes up a lot of space but a wigwam of bamboo canes is ideal for smaller spaces and makes an attractive structure for growing climbing beans.

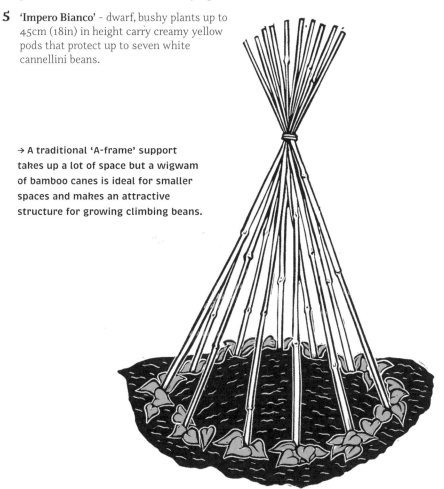

How to Grow Pumpkins & Winter Squash

Pumpkins and closely related winter squashes are native to North America, and played a significant role in the lives of indigenous people. Apart from eating the flesh, the outer shell was used to make containers, while powdered seeds were taken medicinally to fight intestinal infections.

In the kitchen garden, there are loads of tasty varieties worth growing. Fruits come in many shapes, colours and sizes, from tennis-ball to football size. Anything bigger isn't really worth bothering with, unless you want something to carve at Halloween or to enter into a giant vegetable competition.

HOW TO SOW SEEDS

Fill a 7.5cm (3in) pot with peat-free, multipurpose potting compost, firm and level. Make two small holes in the surface and pop a seed into each. Cover with compost, water and add a label for identification - this is essential if you have sown several different varieties.

ENCOURAGE GERMINATION

Slip the pots inside a heated propagator (or cover with small, clear polythene bags) until the seeds have germinated. Shoots can take 5-10 days to appear, depending on the temperature. At this point, remove them from their protected environment and stand the pots on a bright windowsill.

SEEDLING CARE

When the seedlings are around a few centimetres high, evict the weakest of the pair by cutting off the stem at ground level. To avoid a check to growth, move the remaining plant into a slightly larger pot when its roots appear out of the drainage holes in the base. It may be necessary to do this several times before the young plants are ready to go outside.

TIME TO PLANT

Pumpkins and winter squash prefer a sunny, sheltered spot with moisture-retentive soil. The traditional way of growing them is to allow stems to trail across the ground, but varieties with smaller fruit can be trained up a sturdy wigwam of chunky canes or poles. Another option is to raise compact ones in pots.

GROWING AND HARVESTING

Water the plants well, especially during dry spells, and feed every couple of weeks with a fertilizer high in potash. You can help fruit to ripen by removing large leaves that hide it from the sun. Harvest squash when the skin hardens and the remaining foliage starts to die back. Allow the skin to 'cure' in the sun for a couple of weeks before storing in a dark, frost-free place, where pumpkins and winter squash should last for up to six months.

FIVE GREAT PUMPKIN & WINTER SQUASH VARIETIES TO TRY

1 **'Crown Prince'** - an old favourite with squat fruit that is recognizable for its steely blue, ribbed skin and sweet, bright orange flesh.

2 **'Harrier'** - a British-bred butternut squash that stores well; the bushy plants produce four or five pear-shaped fruits that can weigh up 800g (1¾lb) each.

3 **'Jack be Little'** - each plant will produce a dozen or so orange, tennis-ball sized pumpkins that fit snuggly in the palm of a hand.

4 **'Rouge Vif d'Etampes'** - a French heirloom pumpkin with large, flattened and heavily ribbed fruit covered in orange-red skin.

5 **'Turk's Turban'** - dating from the 19th century or earlier, this winter squash has bright orange, hat-shaped fruit flecked that is with red, white and green markings.

→ It's a good idea to insert pumpkins and winter squash seeds into compost so the long edge sits vertically. This will help to reduce the chance of them rotting underground, because water won't build up on the flat surface of the seed. Use this technique for other cucurbits such as cucumber, courgettes and melons, whether planting in pots or the ground.

How to Grow Sweetcorn

Fresh, home-grown sweetcorn eaten within minutes of being harvested is a taste sensation and so much better than any cobs sold in shops. This veg likes a sunny spot and free-draining, moisture-retentive soil. To ensure seeds germinate effortlessly, prepare the ground by creating a seedbed (see page 97).

MALE AND FEMALE FLOWERS

Plants produce both male and female flowers. The tassel-like, male flowers that top plants in summer pollinate the fibrous female flowers which develop on the ends of the cobs below. To become nice and juicy, each kernel needs pollinating individually. If this doesn't happen, the cobs will contain lots of undeveloped kernels.

HOW TO PLANT

To ensure good pollination, it's best to raise sweetcorn plants in square or rectangular blocks, and not in rows. A block of 4 × 5 plants or 5 × 5 plants is ideal. Sow two seeds every 45cm (18in) in 2.5cm (1in)-deep holes. Cover with soil and water. Remove the weakest of each pair of seedlings when they are about 2.5cm (1in) high.

LOOKING AFTER PLANTS

Keep plants well-watered, especially during dry periods, and remove any annual weeds that pop up. As the plants grow, they'll produce aerial roots at the bottom of their stems. Use a draw hoe to cover these exposed roots with soil, helping to give the plants more stability - but take care not to damage the roots.

HARVESTING COBS

Sweetcorn is generally ready for harvesting in late summer, when the silky strands at the end of the cobs turn brown. Check by carefully peeling back the leaves and poking a fingernail into a kernel. If the juice that trickles out is milky, then the cobs are ready to pick. To remove, simply twist the cob away from the plant.

Trivia time

Along with sweetcorn and climbing beans, pumpkins were part of a Three Sisters garden that was planted by native Americans. Essentially an early form of companion planting, beans were allowed to scramble up the tall sweetcorn stalks, while the trailing stems of the squashes smothered the ground, preventing weeds from growing and also retaining moisture in the soil. To native Americans, the three vegetables represented the spirits of three inseparable siblings that would flourish only when grown in close proximity.

EATING AND STORING

Cobs are best eaten immediately because sugars in the kernels turn to starch after picking, affecting their flavour and texture. If you can't eat them in one go, store in the refrigerator for three days. Those with a glut should blanch the cobs in boiling water and allow them to cool before freezing. Consume within 12 months.

THREE GREAT SWEETCORN VARIETIES TO TANTALIZE THE TASTE BUDS

1 'Golden Bantam' - produces sweet and tender yellow cobs; it was launched in 1902.

2 'Summer Glow' - provides bicolour cobs that are packed with yellow and white kernels.

3 'Swift' - is fast to germinate and renowned for its tender kernels.

↓ As it's wind-pollinated, plant sweetcorn seeds in a grid pattern (rather than in single rows) to allow pollen to blow easily from flower to flower.

Grow Crops in Pots

Not so long ago hardly anybody grew crops in pots, but in the past decade or so it has become a popular way to raise all sorts of fruit, vegetables and herbs. Part of its appeal is that it's something anybody can do, whatever the size of their garden. Of course, it's perfect for those with patios, balconies, terraces and really small outdoor spaces.

BEST VEGGIES TO GROW

Among the most suitable veggies for container growing are potatoes, tomatoes, French beans, courgettes, spring onions, Swiss chard, chilli peppers and beetroot, along with stump- or round-rooted varieties of carrots and radish. Mixed salad leaves are a must-grow, especially for beginners, because they'll be ready for harvesting within 21 days of sowing.

FRUIT FOR POTS

There are loads of fruits that will do well in containers. Blueberries, cranberries, figs and gooseberries - along with red, white and blackcurrants - are perfect. Perhaps the best for pots are strawberries - there are close to 100 different varieties available that are supplied as ready-grown plants or rooted runners.

Most fruit trees are too vigorous for pots, but nurserymen have developed some that are propagated by grafting onto dwarfing rootstocks, which restricts their height to around 1.5m (5ft). Apples, pears, plums and cherries, and even more exotic fare such as apricots, peaches and nectarines, are available in this form.

CHOOSING POTS

Pick the right pots for your edibles. It's essential they have drainage holes in the base and are large enough for the eventual size of your plants - anything from 20cm (8in) to 40cm (16in) diameter, depending on what you grow. Plastic pots are good at retaining moisture, while terracotta and ceramic ones dry out far more quickly.

COMPOST

Annual crops will thrive in good-quality, peat-free potting compost that's been fortified with controlled-release fertilizer granules and moisture-retaining crystals. Perennial vegetables and long-lived fruit trees and shrubs prefer something a little more substantial - gritty, soil-based John Innes No 3 compost is ideal.

MAINTENANCE TIPS

The main thing to keep on top of is watering, especially during hot dry spells. If potting compost dries out, it stresses plants, reduces yields and makes them more vulnerable to pests and diseases. Other than that, use a fertilizer high in potash to regularly feed plants that form fruits or pods, from the moment their first flowers appear.

Pest and Disease Watch: Pear Rust

Pear rust is a common fungal disease of pears that results in orange spots on the upper leaf and weird swollen growths on the underside. It's largely cosmetic but can weaken trees over time. There are no sprays available to combat the problem, so pick off and burn infected leaves, and clear up any fallen foliage. The fungal spores overwinter on junipers (*Juniperus*), so consider removing any from gardens to prevent another bout of the disease next year.

'Here's fine rosemary, sage and thyme.

Come buy my ground ivy.

Here's fetherfew, gilliflowers and rue.

Come buy my knotted marjoram, ho!

Come buy my mint, my fine green mint.

Here's fine lavender for your cloaths,

Here's parsley and winter savory,

And heartsease, which all do choose.

Here's balm and hissop and cinquefoil,

All fine herbs, it is well known.

Let none despise the merry, merry cries

Of famous London town!'

(17th-century London street vendor's ballad)

LIGHTS, CAMERA, ACTION!

Britain's great gardens have been lighting up the silver screen for many years. Here are a selection of places that have been used as locations for everything from rom-coms to horror movies.

Groombridge Place, Kent – *The Draughtman's Contract* (1982)

Saltram, Devon – *Sense and Sensibility* (1995)

Kenwood House, London – *Notting Hill* (1999)

The Eden Project, Cornwall – *Die Another Day* (2002)

Stokesay Court, Shropshire – *Atonement* (2007)

Chatsworth House, Derbyshire – *The Wolfman* (2010)

Antony, Cornwall – *Alice in Wonderland* (2010)

Osterley House, London – *The Dark Knight Rises* (2012)

Lacock Abbey, Wiltshire – *Fantastic Beasts* (2017)

Benthall Hall, Shropshire – *Enola Holmes* (2020)

'Out on the lawn I lie in bed,

Vega conspicuous overhead

In the windless nights of June,

As congregated leaves complete

Their day's activity; my feet

Point to the rising moon.'

(W H Auden, *A Summer Night*)

THE MONTH AT A GLANCE

- Trim box topiary (see page 117).
- Remove wayward branches from conifers, along with dead or dying growth (see Prevent Snow Damage to Conifers, page 39).
- Lift and divide congested clumps of primrose (*Primula vulgaris*) and other species (see How to Divide Perennials, page 42).
- Deadhead, feed and water bedding plants (see How to Keep Bedding Plants Going All Summer, page 114).
- Cut back spent flowerheads of early-flowering perennials, to encourage a second flush of flowers in late summer.
- Pick sweet pea flowers regularly, to ensure a constant supply of new blooms.
- Prune early-flowering clematis (see page 117).
- Feed fruiting vegetables with a high-potash feed.
- Set rosemary (*Salvia rosmarinus*) plants in pots or the ground (see How to Grow Rosemary, page 120).
- Plant mint (*Mentha*) in pots (see Grow Mint, page 121).
- Buy and sow courgette seeds (see Quick Courgettes, page 124).
- Sow runner bean seeds (see Sow and Grow Runner Beans, page 126).
- Make an A-frame support for climbing beans (see How to Make an A-frame Support for Beans, page 128).
- Sow mixed salad leaves (see Quick and Easy Salad Leaves, page 121).
- Buy and sow radish seeds (see Sow and Grow Radishes, page 122).
- Sow beetroot seeds (see Sow and Grow Beetroot, page 130).
- Scoop out duckweed from ponds with a small net (see Improve Your Pond, page 78).
- Treat blackspot, remove suckers and combat aphids on roses (see Summer Rose Care, page 118).
- Keep an eye out for lily beetles (see Pest and Disease Watch: Lily Beetles, page 131).
- Fit a water butt (see page 116).

June

It hardly seems possible but the summer solstice arrives this month, and gardeners can spend some long fruitful days outdoors in weather that is often warm, but not fiercely hot or sticky as it can sometimes be later in the season. Of course, a rise in temperature means it's important to water plants regularly, to prevent a check to growth. This is also a fantastic time to be in the garden, with many plants hitting their stride, so ensure that beds, borders and containers turn heads with an array of colourful flowers.

How to Keep Bedding Plants Going All Summer

Normally bursting into life in late spring, bedding plants have the potential to light up gardens until early autumn. Yet ignore petunias, pelargoniums, busy Lizzies (*Impatiens*) and the rest of the tribe, and they'll come to a premature halt. Here's how to get the best out of these colourful plants.

WATERING

Good watering is critical for extending the life of bedding plants. Most are thirsty things that might need watering twice a day to prevent them flagging. Aim to water first thing in the morning or early evening, giving plants plenty of time to soak up moisture with minimal wastage. Don't panic if a container completely dries out. Revive parched plants by standing pots or baskets in a bucket filled with water.

DEADHEADING

Some bedding plants are 'self-cleaning', meaning the flowers naturally drop off as they start to fade, to make room for new ones. However, most cling onto their dying blooms as they want to produce seed pods. At this point, plants divert their energy into making seeds and the floral show will wind down. Therefore, keep plants floriferous by pinching off spent flowers with your thumb and forefinger, or by cutting them off with a pair of plant snips.

FEEDING

In order to ensure strong growth and a succession of flowers, it's important to feed bedding plants often during the growing season. Give plants a weekly pick-me-up with a general-purpose fertilizer, and in late summer switch to feeding them with a fertilizer that's high in potash.

'YOUR LIFE OR YOUR LUPINS'

In a Monty Python sketch set in the 18th century, a highwayman called Dennis Moore breaks into a nobleman's house during the middle of a party. Holding up the guests at gunpoint, he delivers the ultimatum: 'your life or your lupins'. The toffs give up their blooms, and Moore rides off with a bunch that he gives to a peasant couple, whose hovel is full of the flowers. The frustrated husband replies that he's sick of lupins and would rather have something useful like 'gold and silver and clothes and wood and jewels'.

TROUBLESHOOTING

Check bedding plants over on a daily basis. Look out for pests, diseases and weeds, and get to grips with them immediately so there's little or no check to growth. Failure to spot an invasion of aphids, for example, might mean a display comes to a premature halt after just a few weeks. If there are other problems, such as poor growth because of a lack of light or overwatering, then these can be remedied, too.

↓ Remove fading flowers from bedding plants by pinching through the stem with your thumb and forefinger.

Name explain:
Abelia

These summer- into autumn-flowering shrubs are named after Clarke Abel, a botanist on board HMS *Alceste*. A few weeks after leaving China, the ship hit a reef in the Java Sea on 18 February 1817 and started to sink. Everyone on board managed to escape to a nearby island, but Abel lost his plant samples collected in China, including a plant with scented white flowers. Some 27 years later, another sample arrived in Britain and was named *Abelia chinensis* in his honour.

PROJECT: Fit a Water Butt

Water is a precious resource, so it makes sense to install a butt to capture rainwater. Butts come in all shapes and sizes, from huge tanks to slimline models that are perfect for tiny gardens. Access to the water is from a tap fitted to the bottom of the container, and it's best for butts to be placed on a stand to allow space for filling up watering cans underneath. Most people attach butts to the downpipe of a house. However, you could also fix one to a greenhouse, shed or any other garden building with gutters and a downpipe.

YOU WILL NEED

- Water butt ∘ Drill ∘ 2.5cm (1in) flat drill bit ∘ Water butt diverter kit
- Water butt stand ∘ Carpenter's try square ∘ Pencil
- Hacksaw ∘ Stanley knife

HOW TO DO IT

1 Make sure the butt is no more than 50cm (20in) away from the downpipe. Drill a 2.5cm (1in) hole in the water butt using the pre-marked position. Fit a pipe connector to the inside of the butt.

2 Place the butt on the stand and take a level line directly across from the bottom of the connector, and mark the downpipe. Mark a second line 3.5cm (1½in) above. Cut out this section carefully with a hacksaw.

3 Loosen the clamps holding the downpipe, and fit the rainwater diverter. Retighten the clamps. Run a flexible hose between the diverter and connector, cutting it to size with a Stanley knife.

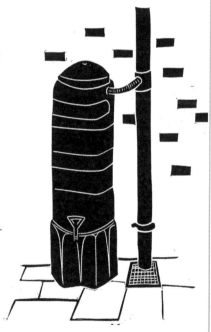

→ **Apart from giving you access to your own supply of water during tough times, rainwater is best for some fussy plants, like blueberries.**

Trim Box Topiary

Held on the first Saturday of June each year, Derby Day is traditionally the time that box (*Buxus*) topiary is given its first cut. Keep secateurs, shears or clippers steady and follow the contours of the shape, which should be visible as a darker area below the new growth. Step back often to check the progress of your work and regularly dip cutting tools into water – this prevents a layer of sap building up on blades and works like a lubricant, allowing blades to cut smoothly.

In the past, it was recommended that you trim box topiary just once more, in autumn. However, many professionals now recommend cutting whenever a sharp silhouette is lost under fresh growth. Not only will this restore a crisp outline, but the topiary shape will also become far denser.

Prune Early-flowering Clematis

Trim clematis that flower before early summer on old wood. Start by removing dead and damaged stems, then cut back stems to keep plants within their allotted space. Finish by securing new shoots to supports. Plants to tackle include *Clematis montana*, *C. alpina* and *C. macropetala*, along with evergreen *C. armandii* and winter-flowering *C. cirrhosa*. Give plants a boost after pruning by sprinkling a general-purpose granular fertilizer over the soil and gently raking it into the surface. Follow with a generous mulch of well-rotted manure or leafmould.

Trim Early-flowering Perennials

As soon as their flowers begin to fade, remove spent spikes from lupins (*Lupinus*), foxgloves (*Digitalis*), delphiniums and mullein (*Verbascum*). Rather than putting all their energy into setting seed, the plants will instead respond by producing a second flush of flowers later in the summer – these are likely to be much smaller, and not as showy as the initial flowers but are welcome all the same. Depending on the plant, either cut the spike right off at the base or else remove it above the nearest set of leaves. Of course, pruning will also leave tidier plants. Finish by giving plants a boost of high-potash fertilizer.

Summer Rose Care

A first-rate rose (*Rosa*) is a thing of great beauty, but there's nothing worse than one that's been neglected. Ensure they remain strong, healthy and floriferous all summer long by giving them some regular attention. Here are my ways to win with roses.

○ Watering is essential during hot dry periods, to prevent flowers from drooping. Ideally, soak the soil first thing in the morning or in the evening, allowing plants to take up moisture before it evaporates. Established roses generally need watering once a week, while newly planted ones may need watering every other day.

○ Mulching will help to slow down moisture loss, as well as keep roots cool and prevent weeds from germinating. Spread a 5cm (2in) layer of composted bark, garden compost or leafmould around the plant, leaving a gap around the stems. Replenish the organic matter every 2-3 months, or whenever it has broken down.

○ Check around the base of roses for suckers. These underground shoots don't have the same characteristics as the rest of the shrub and will sap its energy. Trace the stem back to below the soil surface and twist it off by hand - don't cut it off at ground level as this will stimulate the growth of more suckers.

○ Being high in potassium and phosphorous, Uncle Tom's Rose Tonic is a go-to product with commercial growers. It promotes strong healthy growth rather than lush lanky shoots which are prone to disease. The foliar feed can be sprayed every 7-14 days during the growing season.

○ A common problem faced by owners of roses is blackspot, a fungal disease that results in leaves turning yellow, developing dark patches and falling off branches prematurely. A bad attack will affect vigour, hindering the plant's floral performance. Clear up fallen leaves and spray branches with a suitable fungicide.

Name explain:
PEACE ROSE

Before France fell to Germany in 1940, during the Second World War, an unnamed shrub rose seedling bred by Francis Meilland was sent to the Conard-Pyle Co. nursery in the USA. Boasting sweetly scented, yellow flowers edged with pink, it was named PEACE in 1945. A bloom was given to delegates drafting the United Nations charter in San Francisco of that year, with a note saying: 'We hope the PEACE rose will influence men's thoughts for everlasting world peace.'

- Aphids are attracted to shoot tips, fresh leaves and buds. Their sap sucking can lead to a loss of vigour, distorted stems and wilting, while the sticky substance they excrete on leaves can be infected by sooty mould. Rub them off by hand or spray with an organic pesticide.

ROSES IN THE UK SINGLES CHARTS

- *New Rose* - The Damned (1976) #81
- *Every Rose Has its Thorn* - Poison (1988) #13
- *Roses in the Hospital* - Manic Street Preachers (1993) #15
- *Kiss from a Rose* - Seal (1995) #4
- *Last of the English Roses* - Peter Doherty (2009) #67

Word buster:
Suckers

Vertical shoots that grow from the root system of many trees and shrubs. They often have different characteristics to the parent plant and are therefore considered undesirable in the garden.

↑ Keep a close eye out for suckers and remove as soon as possible to prevent them taking up nutrients and hindering the growth of roses.

How to Grow Rosemary

Native to the Mediterranean region, rosemary (*Salvia rosmarinus*), formely known as Rosmarinus officinalis, has been cultivated for thousands of years and was especially revered by the ancient Greeks, who believed its aroma helped to improve their memories. It arrived in Britain with the Romans and appears frequently in British folklore. For example, during the plague, people stuffed shoots into pouches worn around the neck in the belief that the strong scent would keep them safe from infection.

Common rosemary (*S. rosmarinus*) is the one you are most likely to find, but there are well over 100 different varieties available in the UK. These vary in height, shape and habit, and even in flower colour. Among the best are 'Miss Jessopp's Upright', 'Benenden Blue' and 'Majorca Pink', whose arching branches are clothed with shell-pink blooms in May and June.

Rosemary likes a really sunny, sheltered spot and will flourish in just about any kind of soil so long as it's well-drained. Another option is to plant it in a pot of soil-based potting compost, adding a few handfuls of horticultural grit to open up the mix. Start plants off in containers slightly bigger than their original rootball, moving them into a bigger one each spring. Water plants regularly in summer and feed with a balanced fertilizer once flowers fade.

Plants will earn their keep for a decade or so, providing you prune annually to keep them compact - if you fail to do this, the plants will soon become leggy and misshapen. Simply remove wayward branches or any that spoil the shape of the plant once the floral display is over. Toward the end of a favourite variety's life, propagate plants by taking 10cm (4in)-long semi-ripe cuttings, between mid-summer and early autumn (see page 160).

Trivia time

Founded in 1927, the National Gardens Scheme (NGS) was originally set up to raise funds for retired district nurses. Today, over 3,600 private gardens open annually to visitors and raise money for a number of charities. Since 1932, the details of each garden have been published in the NGS's famous *Garden Visitor's Handbook*, nicknamed the Yellow Book directory.

Quick and Easy Salad Leaves

Mixed salad leaves are one of the easiest and quickest crops you can grow. Sow a few seeds and you will be harvesting handfuls of fresh tasty leaves within just three weeks of sowing. Although salad plants can be grown in the ground, their compact nature and shallow rooting make them an essential edible for containers, such as hanging baskets, pots, window boxes, trays and grow-bags. There's a large range of salad leaves available from seed companies, from fiery mixes containing different types of mustard, sorrel and rocket, to milder blends made up of ingredients like pak choi, chervil and mizuna. Apart from seed mixes, you'll also find individual varieties such as wild rocket and Greek cress.

SOWING AND GROWING

Almost fill your chosen container with peat-free potting compost, leaving a 2.5cm (1in) gap at the top. Press down gently to leave a firm flat surface. Scatter seed across the surface and cover with a layer of sieved compost. Label, water and put the container in a sunny spot. Thin out the seedlings when they are about 2.5cm (1in) tall, following the instructions on the seed packet. Water regularly and take leaves from around the outside of plants, to ensure a succession of fresh new ones. Once plants start to flower, pull them up and put them on the compost heap. For a constant supply of leaves over summer, sow a new pot every three weeks.

Grow Mint

Mint (*Mentha*) is the quintessential summer herb. A handful of crushed leaves are essential for adding zing to a refreshing mojito, while a simple side dish of boiled fresh peas can be turned into something really special when covered in a sprinkling of chopped mint leaves. For your own supply of fresh, aromatic and tangy leaves, snap up some ready-grown plants.

Sadly, mint is a rampant thug that will spread all over the place if planted straight into the ground, so confine plants to 30cm (12in)-wide containers. Place the container in a sunny or partially shaded spot, or plunge it into the soil, making sure the top is above the surface to prevent roots escaping over the rim. Avoid setting different mint varieties too close to each other, because they have a tendency to lose their individual scent and flavour.

Sow and Grow Radishes

Radishes are a summer salad staple, grown for their colour, crunch, piquant flavour and gentle heat. They come in many shapes, colours and sizes. Measuring anywhere from 7.5cm (3in) across to 30cm (12in) long, there are round, torpedo, and long, tapering varieties, in shades of white, yellow, green, red, pink and purple. Radishes are very easy to grow from seed and will thrive in a warm sunny spot. Longer-rooted varieties are best grown in the open ground, while shorter or round-rooted ones can be raised in containers.

Start by preparing a seedbed (see page 97) and then make a 1cm (½in)-deep channel with the corner of a hoe. Leave a gap of 15cm (6in) between rows. Sprinkle seed thinly along the base, cover with soil and water. Germination usually takes 7-10 days. Once the seedlings are large enough to handle, thin them out so the roots have plenty of space to swell - leave one every 2.5cm (1in) or so along the row.

Another option is to sow radish seeds in 30cm (12in)-wide pots of peat-free potting compost. Scatter the seed over the surface and cover with a 1cm (½in) layer of sieved compost.

Radishes will be ready for harvesting in 5-8 weeks - don't leave them any longer or they will turn woody. Lever them up carefully, taking care not to disturb those remaining.

THREE GREAT RADISH VARIETIES

1 'Diana' - produces rounded, two-tone, purple and white roots.

2 'French Breakfast 3' - boasts 5cm (2in)-long, red roots with white tips; it was introduced in 1885.

3 'Red Moon' - developed in Asia, this variety has conical-shaped roots that are rose-pink on both the inside and outside.

A POTTED HISTORY OF RADISHES

Nobody knows for sure, but it's believed that radishes originate from the Mediterranean. They were cultivated by the ancient Romans, Greeks and Egyptians and arrived in Britain at some point during the 1500s. In the 17th century, they were eyed with suspicion, with influential herbalist Nicholas Culpepper warning that anyone accidentally eating radishes should 'send for a physician as fast as you can', to prevent blood poisoning.

HEALTH BENEFITS OF RADISHES

Apart from being low in calories and containing virtually no fat, radishes are a good source of vitamin C and are high in antioxidants.

Feed Fruiting Veg

Apart from plenty of water, many vegetables like a regular feed. Tomatoes, sweet peppers, chilli peppers, aubergines, cucumbers and other fruiting vegetables will all respond well if given a boost every 7-14 days with a liquid or soluble fertilizer that's high in potash. The nutrients will stimulate the plant into developing more flowers and ensure the fruits swell, ripen and are full of flavour. For the best results, feed from the moment the first flowers open until the last fruit has been harvested.

All About Companion Planting

Companion planting is a method of growing two or more different plants together for the beneficial effect they have on a crop you wish to nurture. Flowering plants can be grown with vegetables, to attract pollinating insects, while aromatic plants will disguise the smell of the crop from pests. Some plants can even be grown to attract pests, so they leave desirable edibles alone. There are many tried-and-tested partnerships: grow sweet peas (*Lathyrus odoratus*) alongside climbing beans to attract bees and other pollinators; place pungent marigolds (*Tagetes*) with tomatoes to deter pests; and plant onions with carrots to put off the dreaded carrot fly (see page 87).

(see page 87)

Trivia time

The Beatles spent much of the 1960s in the recording studio but occasionally found time to visit a great garden. In 1965, the Fab Four spent two days at Cliveden, in Berkshire, filming for their movie *Help!*, which included a segment of them frolicking in the estate's bluebell woods. The following May, The Beatles were at Chiswick House in London, where they made two promotional films in the garden for their *Paperback Writer* single and its flipside *Rain*.

'The best place to find God is in a garden. You can dig for him there.'
George Bernard Shaw

Quick Courgettes

Courgettes are one of the easiest, quickest and most productive vegetables you can grow from scratch. Fill a 7.5cm (3in) pot with peat-free potting compost, and then sow two seeds on their sides, 2.5cm (1in) deep. Place in a warm light spot to germinate. When the seedlings are about 2.5cm (1in) tall, tug out the weakest to allow the strongest to grow on.

Plants are ready to go outside once roots poke through the drainage holes in the base of the pot. Set into well-prepared soil, making sure the branches have space to spread 45cm (18in) in all directions, or else move them into 30cm (12in) pots of peat-free potting compost. A further option is to plant two in a grow-bag.

As soon as the first flowers appear, feed the plants weekly with a fertilizer that's high in potash. Water regularly, especially during dry periods - courgettes are thirsty plants that will abort fruiting if subjected to drought. Most plants will remain productive in autumn and will need harvesting about three times a week at the height of summer.

COURGETTE CONUNDRUM

It's an age-old question... will courgettes turn into marrows if left on plants to mature? No, is the answer. Both are members of the same family of plants, but courgettes have been bred specifically for picking at an earlier stage of growth, while marrows are best eaten when fully mature. Courgettes left on plants will simply turn into very large, and unpalatable, courgettes.

FIVE COOL COURGETTE VARIETIES TO TRY

1 **'Black Forest'** - a unique climbing variety with near-black fruit and stems that can be trained vertically up a cane or against trellis.

2 **'Defender'** - is renowned for its heavy crops.

3 **'Orelia'** - produces golden-skinned fruit.

4 **'Rondo di Nizza'** - a heritage variety from Italy that has oval-shaped fruit with a light green skin that's speckled white.

5 **'Safari'** - has dark green skin embellished with light green stripes.

A single courgette plant is capable of producing 30 or so fruit, during its growing season. So, unless you're a complete courgette fanatic, you need grow only one or two plants.

↓ Many varieties of courgette make attractive plants for pots, thanks to their architectural foliage and colourful fruit.

Sow and Grow Runner Beans

Runner beans arrived in Britain from Central America in the 17th century. Back then, they were treated as ornamental climbers, thanks to their flowers and attractive pods. Today, they are the nation's favourite bean to eat. Apart from being darned tasty, runner beans are easy to grow and will provide heavy harvests.

WHERE TO GROW

Runner beans like a sunny spot with moisture-retentive soil. Prepare the ground by removing weeds, digging it over and raking until the texture is fine and crumbly. As runner beans are notoriously greedy plants, enrich the soil with garden compost or well-rotted manure.

SET UP SUPPORTS

Most runner beans need strong supports. A traditional A-frame (see page 128) is ideal for allotments and large veg patches. If space is tight, make a wigwam by placing 5–8 canes in a circle, drawing the tops together and binding with garden twine. Run three horizontal lines of twine around the wigwam, the first 30cm (12in) off the ground and the others evenly spaced up the structure.

GROWING IN THE GROUND

Seeds are ideal for sowing directly into the ground during May and June. Make a 5cm (2in)-deep hole at the foot of each support and drop in two seeds. Cover with soil and water. Once the seeds have germinated, remove the weakest of each pair. As they grow, wind the shoots around the canes and secure with garden twine.

A traditional A-frame (see page 128)

Trivia time

The *Munch Bunch* was a popular series of children's books published in Britain between 1979 and 1984. The books focused on a group of unwanted vegetables, fruits and nuts that ran away from a greengrocer's shop and made their home in an old garden shed. Characters included Dick Turnip, Sally Strawberry and Wally Walnut.

GROWING IN POTS

Not all runner beans are vigorous climbers. Plant breeders have developed a number of varieties that grow to only knee high, making them ideal for large containers. Use 45cm (18in) pots filled with a 30:50 mix of peat-free potting compost and soil-based John Innes No 2. Because of their compact size, these plants don't need supporting.

WATERING ADVICE

Water runner beans frugally in dull weather or while they are establishing, increasing the amount you give them after the first flower buds appear and until the last of the pods have been picked. Mulch the surface of the soil with some garden compost or well-rotted manure, to help lock in moisture and prevent weeds from growing.

AFTERCARE AND HARVESTING

When the stems reach the top of their supports, pinch out the tops to prevent the plants getting overly tall and to ensure they direct their energy into producing more flowers and pods. Runner beans will generally be ready for picking after 12-16 weeks, when 15-20cm (6-8in) long. Snip them off with a pair of scissors.

FIVE GREAT RUNNER BEAN VARIETIES TO TRY

1 **'Enorma'** - red flowers and long, slender pods up to 50cm (20in) long.

2 **'Hestia'** - a compact type with red and white flowers followed by masses of pods.

3 **'Lady Di'** - red flowers and completely stringless, 30cm (12in)-long pods.

4 **'Moonlight'** - has white flowers; bred to produce good crops in any weather.

5 **'Painted Lady'** - a heritage type with red and white flowers followed by 20cm (8in)-long pods.

HEALTH BENEFITS OF RUNNER BEANS

Runner beans are a good source of vitamins A, C and K, and are high in folic acid and fibre.

PROJECT: How to Make an A-frame Support for Beans

Runner beans and other climbing types need strong supports. The traditional way is to construct a beanpole or A-frame structure comprising a double row of bamboo canes held together by a crossbar. The length of the structure depends on available space, but a 2.4m (8ft)-long one is suitable for most veg patches. Ideally, the structure should run in an east-west direction to maximize light levels.

YOU WILL NEED
- Garden measuring tape ∘ 19 x 2.4m (8ft)-long garden canes
- Mallet or hammer ∘ Garden twine

HOW TO DO IT

1 Mark out two straight lines, spaced 45cm (18in) apart.

2 Set nine 2.4m (8ft)-long canes on either side, spacing them 30cm (12in) apart. Drive them 23cm (9in) into the ground at a slight angle, making sure they just overlap at the top.

3 Lay a 2.4m (8ft)-long cane along the top as a crossbar and bind the canes together in a figure-of-eight with twine.

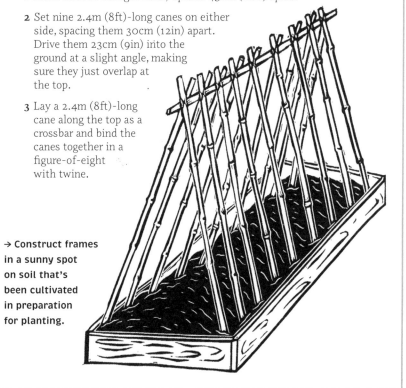

→ Construct frames in a sunny spot on soil that's been cultivated in preparation for planting.

Plant for Bees

The sound of bees buzzing industriously between flowers is synonymous with summer, but some of the UK's 250 different types of bee (24 species of bumblebee, 225 types of solitary bee and one species of honeybee) are active all year round. In order to keep them happy, make sure there are plants to provide nectar and pollen in every season. They go gaga for nectar-rich wild flowers, native shrubs and ornamentals with simple single flowers. Perennials with tube-shaped blooms are a big hit with long-tongued bumblebees. Sadly, bees tend to ignore highly developed ornamentals with double flowers, along with many bedding plants and exotic plants. The following plants are highly attractive to bees:

SPRING
- daphne
- lungwort (*Pulmonaria*)
- primrose (*Primula vulgaris*)
- rosemary (*Salvia rosmarinus*)
- thrift (*Armeria*)

SUMMER
- cinquefoil (*Potentilla*)
- foxglove (*Digitalis*)
- hollyhock (*Alcea*)
- lavender (*Lavandula*)
- mullein (*Verbascum*)

AUTUMN
- abelia
- aster
- ivy (*Hedera*)
- perennial wallflower (*Erysimum*)
- sedum (*Hylotelephium*)

WINTER
- Christmas box (*Sarcococca*)
- hellebore (*Helleborus*)
- mahonia
- snowdrop (*Galanthus*)
- winter aconite (*Eranthis hyemalis*)

Sow and Grow Beetroot

If your experience of beetroot doesn't extend past those jars of limp, crinkle-cut slices swimming in vinegar, then you really need to try some of the fresh stuff. The sweet earthy roots taste great and are remarkably good for you, helping this root veg ascend to superfood status.

HOW TO SOW

Beetroot seed can be sown directly into warm soil outside, any time from mid-April to late June, with globe-shaped beetroot ready to harvest in around 11 weeks and longer-rooted varieties taking closer to four months to reach maturity. Beetroot prefers light, stone-free soil in a sunny spot. Prepare the ground by digging, removing weeds and large stones, and then rake the soil until the texture resembles coarse breadcrumbs. Make a shallow trench, 2.5cm (1in) deep, with a corner of a rake, and then sow two seeds every 10cm (4in). When the seedlings appear, thin out to leave the strongest of each pair.

LOOKING AFTER BEETROOT

Beetroot is very easy to look after. Keep the area around plants free from weeds and water crops regularly, especially during dry spells - this helps the roots swell to full size, along with preventing them from splitting and turning woody. It also stops the beetroot plants running to seed prematurely. The good news is that no feeding is necessary.

LIFTING THE CROP

Harvest the roots while they are young and tender - roots left in the ground to mature tend to split or turn woody. Grasp the foliage firmly where it meets the top of the root and pull from the ground. After lifting, twist off the foliage about 2.5cm (1in) above the root. Don't cut the leaves because this results in the roots 'bleeding' red sap and turning soft.

TOP TIP

Beetroot seeds are a cluster of up to six seeds held within a dried fruit case, which contains a natural chemical that inhibits seed germination. To improve the germination rate, soak seeds in warm water for about 30 minutes prior to sowing.

THREE BRILLIANT BEETROOT VARIETIES TO TRY

1 **'Burpee's Golden'** - introduced in the 1940s, this variety from the USA has burned-orange skin and golden flesh with a sweet mild flavour.

2 **'Chioggia'** - developed in market gardens around Venice prior to the 1840s, the pink-skinned roots of this variety reveal dark red and white rings when sliced open.

3 **'Cylindra'** - a Danish variety that first appeared in the early 1800s and has long, slim, cylindrical, dark pink roots that are perfect for slicing.

Pest and Disease Watch: Lily Beetles

Lilies (*Lilium*), fritillaries (*Fritillaria*) and other members of the lily family are vulnerable to attack by lily beetles - shiny scarlet pests with black heads that can defoliate plants, giving them a tatty appearance. Check plants daily for adult beetles, their clusters of red eggs and their larvae, which are encased in their own black, jelly-like excrement. Pick the beetles off by hand, taking care not to drop them as they are hard to find when they fall on their backs.

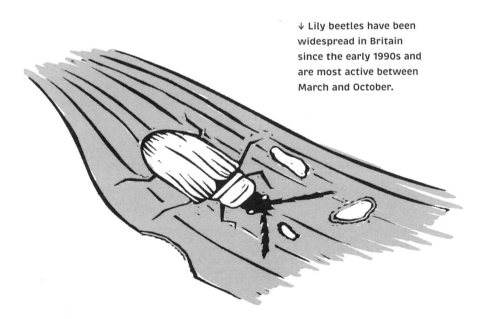

↓ Lily beetles have been widespread in Britain since the early 1990s and are most active between March and October.

'A boat, beneath a sunny sky,

Lingering onwards dreamily

In an evening of July –'

(Lewis Carroll, *A Boat Beneath a Sunny Sky*)

THE MONTH AT A GLANCE

- Prune forsythia and other early-flowering shrubs (see Prune Early-flowering Shrubs, page 134).
- Summer prune wisterias (see How to Prune Wisteria, page 136).
- Deadhead rose flowers as they start to fade.
- Remove sideshoots from bamboos (see Enhance the Beauty of Bamboos, page 146).
- Sprinkle some general granular fertilizer around asters and other late-flowering perennials, to ensure a great display.
- Water camellias, rhododendrons and magnolias (see page 143).
- Plant out seedlings in the garden before they get too leggy.
- Support sunflowers (*Helianthus annuus*) with stout canes, securing stems every 30cm (12in) with soft twine.
- Plant thyme (*Thymus*) (see Tips for Growing Thyme, page 139).
- Remove flowers from herbs, to ensure they continue to produce more leaves.
- Thin out apple and pear fruit (see page 144).
- Trim summer-fruiting strawberries after picking the last of the fruit (see End-of-Season Care, page 81).
- Ensure grapes ripen by removing some of the leaves hiding bunches, allowing sunlight to reach the fruit.
- Use a hoe to draw up soil around the base of sweetcorn plants, to improve stability (see How to Grow Sweetcorn, page 108).
- Check cabbages and other leafy vegetables for caterpillars.
- Top up ponds if the water level drops in warm weather.
- Sprinkle compost heaps with water in dry weather.
- Mulch wall-grown shrubs and climbers with bark, garden compost or leafmould, to keep their roots moist (see Mulch Soil, page 26).
- Control vine weevils (see Pest and Disease Watch: Vine Weevil, page 143).
- Move houseplants outside (see Give Houseplants a Summer Holiday, page 140).
- Raise humidity around houseplants (see page 141).

July

Summer is now in full swing, and this is the month to kick back and really enjoy your garden. Warm sunny days are ideal for relaxing, tucking into al fresco meals and getting together with friends and family. It doesn't matter whether you've got a tiny plot or a few rolling hectares, make sure you have somewhere comfortable to take the weight off your feet. You don't need anything fancy - a simple blanket set down on the lawn will do. Don't forget to provide some shade as the sun can be ferocious.

Prune Early-flowering Shrubs

Deciduous shrubs that flower between spring and early summer generally bloom on wood produced the previous year. These plants should be pruned soon after the floral display is over, to avoid removing dormant buds. Pruning will also keep shrubs within bounds and ensure flowers are produced on new branches within clear view, where they are easy to enjoy. If left, plants will become lanky and flowers will be held higher up the plant.

Whatever shrubs you have to tackle, always start by removing the three Ds – dead, diseased and dying wood. Also, take out thin wispy shoots and the odd older branch, to ease congestion. All of this will help to improve the health of the shrub by increasing the amount of light and air that can reach the centre. Then trim the shrub so that it possesses an open, vase-like shape which is more slender at the bottom than at the top. To do this, prune wayward stems that spoil the outline and cut back branches that cross or rub against each other. Always prune to an outward-facing bud, using a 45-degree cut slanted away from the bud.

10 SHRUBS TO PRUNE AFTER FLOWERING

- beauty bush (*Kolkwitzia amabilis*)
- deutzia
- *Exochorda × macrantha*
- flowering currant (*Ribes sanguineum*)
- flowering quince (*Chaenomeles japonica*)
- *Forsythia × intermedia*
- lilac (*Syringa vulgaris*)
- mock orange (*Philadelphus*)
- spiraea
- weigela

Name explain: Miss Willmott's Ghost

Ellen Willmott was one of the country's most revered horticulturists in the late 19th century. Described by her contemporary Gertrude Jekyll as 'the greatest of all living gardeners', she was among the first recipients of the prestigious Victoria Medal of Honour, launched by the RHS in 1897. During the latter part of her life, Ellen became increasingly eccentric and would furtively sow seeds of *Eryngium giganteum* in other people's gardens. She did this so often during her lifetime that, by the time she died in 1934, this dramatic, short-lived perennial with spiky, silvery white flowerheads had been dubbed Miss Willmott's ghost.

In 2011, pop queen Madonna was given a freshly cut hydrangea stem by a fan. The star was not impressed. She rolled her eyes, dropped the flower to the floor and muttered: 'I absolutely loathe hydrangeas.' A week later she released a tongue-in-cheek video on YouTube called Madonna's 'Love Letter to Hydrangeas'. Shot as a black-and-white silent film, she starts by caressing and apologizing to a bunch of hydrangeas. It's all an act. She throws them to the ground and stamps on them, while an on-screen caption states that she still hates hydrangeas and always will do.

↓ If left to their own devices many early-flowering shrubs, like forsythia, become overly tall with flowers held on the tops of branches. Ensure plants remain floriferous and shapely by pruning immediately after flowering. Step back often to check on your progress and to ensure you are left with an attractive, vase-like shape.

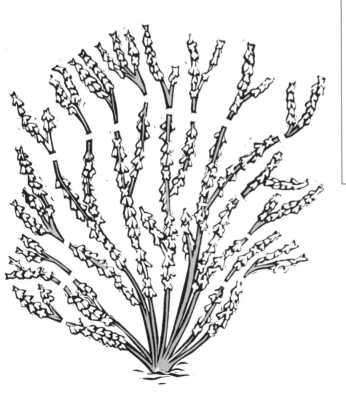

How to Prune Wisteria

Wisteria will grow rampantly if left to its own devices, producing masses of leafy growth at the expense of flowers. Pruning is necessary to divert the plant's energy from making foliage into producing flower buds. It also reduces the mass of whippy shoots and so helps light reach the network of branches inside. As a rule, plants need trimming twice a year – first in July followed by a second cut in February. In July, reduce all of the leafy shoots produced from the older stems during the current season to five or six leaves. In February, shorten all the sideshoots you pruned before, leaving two or three buds on each.

→ **Use secateurs to reduce the length of sideshoots, working methodically across the plant – it may be necessary to use a ladder or hedge cutting platform, depending on the height of the climber.**

TWISTED FACT

Chinese wisteria (*Wisteria sinensis*) and its varieties twine around supports in an anticlockwise manner, while Japanese wisteria (*W. floribunda*) winds clockwise.

Attract More Butterflies

Butterflies are beautiful insects that bring colour and movement to gardens, as well as helping to pollinate plants and acting as an indicator of a healthy ecosystem. Sadly, many species are in decline, but gardeners can assist their plight by turning outdoor spaces into havens for these flying creatures. The key to attracting butterflies is to pick plants with flowers high in nectar, to provide them with energy. Make sure there are some to provide this source of food from spring until the end of autumn, when butterflies build up their reserves for winter. Relaxing the upkeep of the rest of your garden will help butterflies to prosper. Avoid using pesticides and don't be in a rush to evict weeds. Bittercress (*Cardamine*), clover (*Trifolium*) and dock (*Rumex*) are the main food plants of several species, while red admirals, commas, small tortoiseshells and peacocks like to lay their eggs on stinging nettles (*Urtica*), which are then eaten by their ravenous caterpillars. Butterflies naturally roost in trees, grasses or among the shoots of climbing plants, and they hibernate within the cracks of a wall, corner of a shed or garage over winter. Give them another option by installing a butterfly nesting box against a sunny wall or fence.

BUTTERFLY FACT FILE

- There are 57 different butterflies resident in the UK, along with two regular migrant species. Of these, 22 are regularly found in British gardens.

- There are several collective nouns for a group of butterflies. Among them are flight, flutter and kaleidoscope.

- Butterflies actually have four wings, and not two.

- People who study butterflies are known as lepidopterists.

- The average lifespan for most butterfly species is around 2-4 weeks, although adult brimstones can live for up to ten months.

- In the past 150 years, five butterfly species have become extinct in Britain: the large copper; mazarine blue; black-veined white; large blue; and large tortoiseshell.

- In Greek and Roman mythology, butterflies were a symbol of immortality.

GREAT PLANTS FOR BUTTERFLIES

Pick a selection of different plants to attract a wide range of butterflies:

SHRUBS

- buddleia
- California lilac (*Ceanothus*)
- hebe
- lavender (*Lavandula*)
- lilac (*Syringa*)

PERENNIALS

- Michaelmas daisy (*Aster*)
- red valerian (*Centranthus ruber*)
- sedum (*Hylotelephium*)
- *Verbena bonariensis*
- yarrow (*Achillea*)

ANNUALS AND BIENNIALS

- aubretia
- honesty (*Lunaria*)
- sweet William (*Dianthus barbatus*)
- violets (*Viola*)
- wallflower (*Erysimum*)

↑ A wide range of butterflies are drawn toward the scented flowers of buddleias.

Tips for Growing Thyme

Thyme (*Thymus*) is an indispensable culinary herb and so easy to grow in the garden that there's no need to buy those jars of dusty dried leaves from the supermarket. Apart from the bog standard culinary thyme (*T. vulgaris*), there are hundreds of other varieties available, ranging from prostrate carpeting types to small upright shrubs up to 30cm (12in) tall. Thyme leaves vary enormously in size, fragrance and appearance, with a few boasting variegated foliage. These plants prefer a sunny spot with free-draining soil, or can be raised in containers. Start them off in 15cm (6in) pots filled with soil-based John Innes No 1 compost, adding extra grit to enhance drainage. Thymes don't require feeding but they will benefit from the occasional drink, even though they are drought-tolerant. Keep them compact and looking tidy by trimming lightly in summer, once their flowers fade. Selectively remove entire shoots from culinary thymes, aiming to retain an attractive shape.

THYME FOLKLORE

Largely native to hot dry parts of southern and western Europe, thyme was probably brought to Britain by the Romans. It has long been part of our folklore. Sprigs of thyme were given to knights to bring them good luck in battle, and on St Luke's Day, in October, young women would spread a thyme-based paste over their bodies before going to bed in the hope that their future husband would be revealed in a dream.

THREE GREAT THYME VARIETIES TO TRY

1 *T. herba-barona* 'Lemon-scented' is a mat-forming variety, collected by the late Beth Chatto, a renowned plantswoman, in Corsica, whose leaves are ideal for giving a citrus kick to food.

2 *T. pulegioides* 'Archer's Gold' forms a short, 45cm (18in)-wide mat of golden yellow leaves with a distinctive lemon scent. It was discovered in Somerset, England.

3 *T. pulegioides* 'Foxley' has broad green leaves with distinctive cream margins, which clothe 15cm (6in)-tall stems topped with mauve flowers in late spring and early summer.

Give Houseplants a Summer Holiday

If your houseplants are looking a bit unhappy, give them a summer airing in the garden. Higher light levels will encourage lots of healthy growth and fresh moving air will discourage a flare-up of fungal diseases. The odd shower will wash dust off plant foliage, helping to improve photosynthesis.

ACCLIMATIZE PLANTS

As they are used to low light levels indoors, plants often suffer from scorch when immediately set in a bright position. So, acclimatize plants slowly to life outdoors by starting them in a shady, sheltered spot and gradually increasing the amount of light they receive on a daily basis until you display them in their final position in the garden.

LIGHT LEVELS

Make sure you give plants the right amount of light to avoid a check to growth. Succulents including cacti, scented-leaf pelargoniums, citrus plants and Chinese hibiscus (*Hibiscus rosa-sinensis*) like a sunny spot. Spider plants (*Chlorophytum*), Begonia rex, Swiss cheese plants (*Monstera deliciosa*), Cape primrose (*Streptocarpus*) and peace lilies (*Spathiphyllum wallisii*) will thrive in a shadier position.

LOOKING AFTER HOUSEPLANTS

Feed houseplants occasionally to ensure they produce lush healthy growth and check them often for slugs, caterpillars and other pests. Houseplants will require regular watering when they are outside because the compost will dry out quickly during sunny spells and in breezy weather. Move plants to a sheltered spot during prolonged wet periods.

**Word buster:
Shed**

First recorded in 1481 as *shadde*, possibly a variant of the word shade. The word shade comes from the Old English *sceadu*, meaning 'shade, shadow, darkness'.

MOVING HOUSEPLANTS BACK INDOORS

Protect plants from cooler temperatures by preparing them for a move back indoors in early autumn. Over a week or so, bring them in at night, returning them to the garden by day. Once they've been conditioned, remove any dead leaves and flowers, and inspect them carefully to avoid bringing in pests.

RAISING HUMIDITY AROUND HOUSEPLANTS

Many houseplants come from tropical parts of the world and flourish in humid conditions. An easy way of raising humidity around vulnerable houseplants is to mist them regularly with a hand-held sprayer - simply spritz until it looks as if a fine dew has settled on the leaves. As a rule, it's best to treat plants first thing in the morning, so they can enjoy the benefits of misting during the day and the leaves are dry when evening arrives.

FIVE HOUSEPLANTS THAT LIKE MISTING

1 croton (*Codiaeum variegatum*)

2 flamingo flower (*Anthurium*)

3 parlour palm (*Chamaedorea elegans*)

4 peace lily (*Spathiphyllum wallisii*)

5 umbrella tree (*Schefflera arboricola*)

Trivia time

At the RHS Chelsea Flower Show 2009, TV presenter James May with three other collaborators created a garden out of Plasticene, which featured on his series *James May's Toy Stories*. 'Paradise In Plasticene' was given a special gold medal made of Plasticene by RHS judges and won the People's Choice award.

'My garden is my most beautiful masterpiece.'

Claude Monet

Holiday Care Tips

July is the start of the great summer getaway for many Brits, who leave their gardens to fend for themselves while relaxing for a week or two. Nobody wants to return to find their outdoor space in a sorry state, so give your garden a little bit of attention before packing your suitcase.

SORT BEDS AND BORDERS

Beds and borders can go downhill quickly in your absence, so spend a few minutes snipping off fading flowers from shrubs and perennials, and hoicking out any large weeds by hand. Despatch weed seedlings with a hoe. Water the ground and cover with a 7.5cm (3in) layer of mulch, to lock in moisture and prevent weeds returning.

MOW THE LAWN

Give your lawn a trim the day before you go away. Set mower blades slightly lower than normal so the lawn doesn't look too shaggy when you come home. Trim any grass overhanging edges with a pair of long-handled edging shears. Finish by giving the lawn a good soak, in case there is dry weather in the next week or so.

PLANTS IN POTS

Anything growing in a container is vulnerable to drying out during a sunny spell. In order to slow down the process, move containers to a shadier position and give them a good soaking the night before you head off. Another option is to set up an automatic irrigation system programmed to come on for five minutes in the morning and evening.

FRUIT AND VEGETABLES

Many crops reach their peak in mid-summer and if not harvested plants will soon run out of steam. Nip around the veg patch on the day before your holiday begins and pick anything that is ripe or almost ripe. Alternatively, give a neighbour the opportunity to help themselves to your food in return for occasionally watering the crops.

KEEP GREENHOUSES COOL

Temperatures can build up rapidly in greenhouses over summer, even if you have covered the outside with shade paint or fixed shade netting to the inside. Keep things cool by leaving doors, windows and vents open. Prevent pots from drying out by standing them on a piece of damp capillary matting placed on the bottom of a seed tray.

Water Camellias, Magnolias and Rhododendrons

Keep rhododendrons, azaleas and camellias well-watered during dry spells in mid- to late summer, to encourage next spring's flower buds to form. If plants are allowed to dry out, the buds are likely to drop early next year before they have a chance to open. These plants prefer slightly acidic water, such as rainwater stored in a butt. Tap water is more alkaline because of its calcium content. It's fine to give occasionally to parch the thirst of these plants, but avoid frequent usage.

Pest and Disease Watch: Vine Weevil

Adult vine weevil beetles remove U-shaped notches around the outside of leaves. The damage is unsightly but purely cosmetic. However, the beetles lay eggs in the ground, which hatch into C-shaped, white grubs that sever roots. If you spot foliage damage, place newspaper under the plants and give them a good shake – the beetles should fall onto the paper and can then be destroyed. Kill their grubs by soaking the soil with Nemasys Vine Weevil Killer, an organic control best applied between March and November.

↓ Adult vine weevils tend to feed at night, gnawing U-shaped holes from around the margins of leaves.

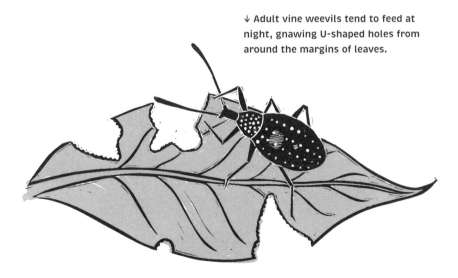

Thin Out Apple and Pear Fruit

Apples and pears will naturally drop some baby fruit to the ground if clusters are overcrowded – this is a tree's way of ensuring the remaining fruit has plenty of room to expand. Although this phenomenon is known as 'June drop', the process can actually take place at any point from late May until July. It's usually necessary to follow up this natural shedding yourself in July by carrying out some extra thinning by hand, to give developing fruits sufficient space to reach their correct size. First remove small or misshapen fruit, including the large central 'king' apple if it is damaged. Less thinning is generally necessary for pears.

↓ Either use narrow-bladed garden snips to thin out developing fruit or grasp firmly between your fingers and pull backwards so the stem snaps off cleanly.

Grow Hardy Succulents

Mention succulents and most people will think of tender plants grown as houseplants. However, there's a group of hardier ones that will take a cold snap in their stride. Among them are houseleeks (*Sempervivum*), carpobrotus and delosperma, along with some sedums (*Hylotelephium*), crassulas and aloes. These plants are incredibly versatile. They are obvious candidates for containers, while larger ones make great specimens for xeriscape schemes. Smaller ones that gradually spread to form compact mounds are perfect in rock gardens or planted in alpine schemes; they can also be used to form living walls and green roofs.

As a general rule, hardy succulents prefer a warm sunny spot and like very well-drained soil. Use soil-based potting compost, such as John Innes No 2 with a handful of extra grit, if growing them in pots. Water occasionally in summer and remove any dead leaves, stems or rosettes.

TEN OF THE BEST HARDY SUCCULENTS TO TRY

1 *Aloe striatula*

2 *Carpobrotus edulis*

3 *Crassula sarcocaulis*

4 *Delosperma cooperi* Wheels of Wonder Series

5 *Graptopetalum paraguayense*

6 *Sedum spathulifolium* 'Cape Blanco'

7 *Sedum spurium* 'Schorbuser Blut'

8 *Sedum takesimense* ATLANTIS

9 *Sempervivum arachnoideum*

10 *Sempervivum* 'Othello'

Trivia time

According to the Horticultural Trades Association, three million people in the UK took up gardening for the first time during the coronavirus lockdown of 2020.

Enhance the Beauty of Bamboos

Bamboos are hard to beat for year-round colour, structure and style, but if you ignore these architectural beauties they'll lose their appeal. Fortunately, it's easy to keep bamboo plants in great shape by giving them a little bit of attention.

Thin out congested clumps by cutting dead or thin canes flush with the ground. Not only will this improve the clump's appearance by making it seem less solid, but it will also encourage healthy growth by allowing light and air to penetrate.

In order for attractive canes to be properly enjoyed, strip the leafy sideshoots away from the bottom third of the entire clump. During the growing season, this is easy to do by hand, snapping them off with a swift downward movement.

Bamboos shed a lot of leaf sheaths on the ground as they grow. Rake some of these up, to smarten the appearance of the bamboos, but don't be overly zealous with tidying - the material is high in silica, which helps to strengthen the canes.

As they grow taller, many bamboos bow under the weight of their foliage. If canes fall in the way of a path or become so wayward that they spoil the shape of the plant, simply snip off the top to reduce the weight and they will bounce upright.

If you have the patience and a lot of free time on your hands, you could even polish the stems. Some professional growers rub individual stems with a soft cloth moistened with vegetable oil, before exhibiting bamboos at flower shows.

DID YOU KNOW ?

Despite their head for heights, bamboos are officially members of the grass family. Native to tropical parts of southeast and south Asia, dragon bamboo (*Dendrocalamus giganteus*) can put on 40cm (16in) of growth a day. One specimen in Arunachal Pradesh state in northeast India measured in at 42m (137.9ft), making it the tallest grass in the world.

↓ Young sideshoots are easy to remove from bamboos by hand, using a swift downward motion. Older sideshoots are much firmer and need to be taken off with secateurs.

'There comes a warning like a spy

A shorter breath of Day

A stealing that is not a stealth

And Summers are away.'

(Emily Dickinson, *There Comes a Warning Like a Spy*)

THE MONTH AT A GLANCE

- Plant bulbs (see Plant Autumn-flowering Bulbs, page 150).
- Prevent top-heavy shoots of dahlias from toppling, by securing them with a stout cane.
- Trim evergreen hedges.
- Prune lavender (*Lavandula*) as flowers fade (see Prune Lavender, page 153).
- Prune apple and pear trees (see Prune Apple and Pear Trees, page 156).
- Collect seeds from perennials (see Collect Seeds, page 159).
- Take semi-ripe cuttings (see Take Semi-ripe Cuttings, page 160).
- Sow parsley seeds (see Grow Parsley, page 154).
- Buy and sow rocket seeds (see Grow Rocket, page 158).
- Preserve herbs by drying and freezing (see Preserve Herbs, page 152).
- Water tomato plants twice a day during hot spells, to prevent blossom end rot.
- Harvest courgettes regularly, to prevent fruit from becoming tough and woody.
- Help pumpkins and winter squash to ripen by removing large leaves that hide fruit from the sun.
- Sow spring onion seeds (see page 157).
- Buy and sow Swiss chard seeds (see page 164).
- Lift onions from the soil when leaves have withered and turned a straw-brown colour.
- Snip off dying leaves from waterlilies (*Nymphaea*), to prevent them from discolouring ponds.
- Prevent the spread of brown rot fungal disease on apple trees by removing fruit with soft brown patches on the skin.
- Top up birdbaths regularly during warm weather.

August

Long, hot summer days are ideal for chilling in the garden, so make the most of good weather during the day - evenings can also be very warm and a few carefully placed lights will ensure you can remain outdoors long after the sun has gone down. There are vegetables to sow and a bit of husbandry to attend to, but don't overdo it. August is predominantly about enjoying having an outdoor space.

Plant Autumn-flowering Bulbs

Everybody knows spring-flowering bulbs, but there's a lesser-known group that will add a pop of colour to gardens in autumn. Bulbs, corms and tubers of autumn daffodil (*Sternbergia lutea*), colchicum, scilla, autumn crocus and autumn snowflake (*Acis autumnalis*) will bloom from September to November, depending on the variety. Late-flowering bulbs like a sunny spot and well-drained soil. They are ideal for growing at the front of beds and borders, setting alongside paths and dotting into rock gardens - colchicums and crocus are excellent for naturalizing in grass. Set scillas 7.5cm (3in) deep and autumn daffodils 12cm (5in) deep. Plant other types at a depth of three times their own size. For a really impressive display, arrange in groups of five or more, spacing bulbs 7.5-30cm (3-12in) apart, according to what you are growing.

FIVE AUTUMN-FLOWERING BULBS TO TRY

1 **autumn daffodil** (*Sternbergia lutea*) - dazzles in September and October with its yellow flowers held on 15cm (6in) stems.

2 **autumn snowflake** (*Acis autumnalis*) - bears nodding white flowers on 23cm (9in)-tall stems during September.

3 **autumn squill** (*Scilla autumnalis*) - carries bright blue flowers on wiry, 12cm (5in)-high stems from late August into October.

4 *Crocus speciosus* **'Conqueror'** - standing at just 15cm (6in) in height, the deep blue flowers appear during October and November.

5 *Crocus speciosus* **'Oxonian'** - rounded, dark violet-blue flowers, measuring up to 10cm (4in) across, arrive in mid- or late autumn.

THE HEALING POWERS OF ECHINACEAS

Long before echinaceas were admired by gardeners for their flowers, the plants were highly regarded by Native American tribes. The Sioux, Blackfoot and Cheyenne considered echinacea a medicinal one-stop shop, using roots to treat toothache, snakebites, coughs, burns, sexually transmitted diseases and countless other ailments. Early settlers embraced its use, and it remained a folk remedy until 1880, when the first mass-market product containing echinacea was launched. Today, echinacea capsules are widely taken to fight off common colds.

LIFE CYCLE OF AUTUMN-FLOWERING BULBS

Most autumn-flowering bulbs have the same life cycle. After planting in late summer, plants quickly produce flowers on bare stems without leaves. Once these wither, they develop underground, leading to a clump of foliage appearing in spring. These will die back in early summer as the plant enters a short period of dormancy before flowering again the following autumn.

ALL ABOUT COLCHICUMS

Colchicums are autumn-flowering bulbs that are native to parts of Africa, Asia and Europe. One species, however, can be found growing wild in Britain – *C. autumnale*, which bears lavender-pink flowers and is largely confined to meadowland around southern and central England. As well as the genus botanical name (which derives from Colchis, an ancient kingdom that was located in modern-day Georgia), these autumn-flowering bulbs have several common names, including naked ladies, meadow saffron and autumn crocus. Plant corms 10cm (4in) deep in late summer, and their flowers will then add pops of colour from September to November, depending on the variety.

Among the best are:

° **C. × agrippinum** - introduced in the early 20th century, this has soft lilac flowers overlaid with a darker shade in a chequerboard pattern.

° **C. autumnale 'Album'** - standing on 15cm (6in)-tall stalks, the goblet-shaped blooms are pure white.

° **C. 'Waterlily'** - produces 10cm (4in)-wide, fully double, lilac flowers.

° **C. 'Harlekijn'** - flowers shaped like a jester's hat have pointed, amethyst -violet petals with white tips.

A WORD OF WARNING:

All parts of the colchicum plant are toxic, so wear gloves when planting corms or wash your hands thoroughly after handling.

↓ **Double-flowered Colchicum 'Waterlily'.**

Fill the Hungry Gap

These days, the term hungry gap describes a period in early spring when pickings of fruit and vegetables are lean. In bygone times, it was about a six-week stretch of great hardship for country folk as stored crops and grains were running low, and any vegetables started in early spring were a long way off from being ready. Today, it has no impact on our lives thanks to 24-hour supermarkets selling out-of-season crops, but gardeners can still bridge the hungry gap by planting plugs or young plants, or sowing seeds of hardy crops. Among the most suitable crops are spinach, Swiss chard, leeks, spring cabbage, broad beans, kale and some Oriental edibles.

Preserve Herbs

Many herbs are annuals that will soon give up the ghost, or else they are perennials that will die back as colder weather sets in.

A good way of preserving the leaves of basil (*Ocimum*), tarragon (*Artemisia dracunculus*), oregano (*Origanum*) and other herbs is to dry them before they disappear. Snip off a handful of fresh shoots and dip this in a bowl of water, to remove any dirt. Dry with a kitchen towel. Cover a tray with a sheet of paper, lay the shoots on top and place in an airing cupboard until the herbs are dry. Remove individual leaves and put them in small bags. Secure the tops of the bags to keep the herbs fresh, label and store in a kitchen cupboard.

Another option is to freeze herbs. Harvest the shoots when they are young and chop leaves into small pieces. Half-fill an ice-cube tray with water, pack herbs into each compartment and put in the freezer. Once frozen, the cubes can be stored in freezer bags for convenience.

Trivia time

Adam the Gardener is a cartoon character who appeared in a popular comic strip published by the *Sunday Express* during the 1940s. Written by journalist Morley Adams and drawn by Cyril Cowell, Adam provided weekly gardening advice for readers. Sadly, not all of his tips have stood the test of time. For example, Adam recommended getting rid of cutworms using Paris Green, a highly toxic green substance that contained arsenic. He didn't implore those using it to wear gloves, only to 'wash hands after, due to its poisonous nature'.

TOP TIP

When choosing stems of herbs to dry, avoid older woody shoots as the flavour will be poorer than that of fresher stems.

Prune Lavender

Without regular pruning, a neat, compact and floriferous lavender (*Lavandula*) will turn into an untidy woody shrub that flowers poorly. The key is to trim twice a year, rather than the traditional once. Give lavenders their first cut immediately after flowering, removing the spent flower stems and around 2cm (¾in) of growth, to retain an attractive rounded shape. Prune plants again lightly in early spring if they are looking a bit untidy.

Anyone who has grown lavender will have been warned not to cut back into old wood, which makes restoring overgrown plants almost impossible. While it is true that lavenders are reluctant to produce fresh growth from woody stems, it is possible to cut into them if any embryonic shoots are present – simply cut back to the new growth.

↑ **When pruning lavender plants keep a close eye out for adult rosemary beetles and their larvae (see page 165).**

Grow Parsley

Parsley (*Petroselinum*) is an indispensable culinary herb that comes in two main forms: flat and curly-leaved. Both can be sown now for leaves that will be ready for harvesting in autumn. As this herb is notoriously slow to get going from seed, speed up the germination process by soaking the seeds in water overnight. When you are ready, scatter seed thinly over a large pot filled with peat-free potting compost, aiming to leave about 2.5cm (1in) between each seed – don't worry if some are closer, as you can thin them out later. Cover with a 1cm (½in) layer of finely sieved compost and water gently. Put the pot in a sheltered spot to allow the seeds to germinate – a cold frame, greenhouse, front porch or a similar place is ideal. Another option is to sow the seed in 1cm (½in)-deep trenches in the ground. Cover the seed with soil and water.

Thin out seedlings when they are large enough to handle, leaving about 2.5cm (1in) between plants. Keep the plants well-watered and feed every couple of weeks with a balanced liquid fertilizer. Harvest parsley as required by cutting off stems with scissors and immediately remove any flowerheads that appear, to extend its cropping life.

THREE GREAT PARSLEY VARIETIES TO TRY

1 'Envy' - dark green, densely curled leaves.

2 'Laura' - dark green, flat leaves that have an intense flavour.

3 'Plain Leaved 2' - a flat-leaved variety with a strong flavour.

THE DEVIL'S HERB

An old superstition suggests that parsley is the Devil's herb, and according to a mid-17th-century proverb: 'Parsley seed goes nine times to the Devil'. This alludes to parsley being tricky to grow and that seeds would need to be sown nine times before any would germinate. In reality, parsley seeds can sometimes take up to six weeks to germinate but will do so if the soil conditions are right. It's likely its bad reputation comes from seeds failing in cold wet soil or because the seeds were simply old and no longer viable.

HEALTH BENEFITS OF PARSLEY

Parsley contains iron and vitamins A, C and E, along with the antioxidant apigenin.

PROJECT: Make a Gravel Garden

Gravel gardens are high-impact, low-maintenance features that allow you to grow a range of drought-tolerant plants.

YOU WILL NEED

○ Edging material ○ 10mm (½in) gravel ○ Rake ○ Trowel
○ Drought-tolerant plants

HOW TO DO IT

1 Whether you are making a gravel garden from scratch or a replacing an existing feature, start by removing weeds, turf and any other vegetation.

2 Add a solid edge around the outside if necessary, to retain the gravel and allow it to be spread at a consistent depth.

3 Pick a type of gravel that complements existing landscaping features or that comes from the local area, to ensure it suits its surroundings - stone that's around 10mm (½in) in diameter is ideal.

4 Spread a 5-7.5cm (2-3in) layer of gravel over the soil and rake level. Some people prefer to lay the gravel on landscape material but this stymies self-seeding and doesn't allow the gravel to work its way into the soil, which improves drainage.

5 Scrape back some gravel by hand and make a shallow hole in the soil for the base of each rootball. Pop in the plant, fill any gaps in the hole with soil and pull back the gravel until the rootball is covered. Note: When setting plants in gravel gardens, it's important that the crowns are flush with the surface of the gravel and not with the soil.

MAINTAINING A GRAVEL GARDEN

○ Water newly planted specimens regularly during warm dry weather, to prevent the rootballs drying out while the plants become established.
○ Pull out any obvious weeds and edit self-seeded perennials.
○ Rake the surface of the gravel garden when necessary, to keep it even.
○ Keep a bag or two of gravel in storage, to top up surface levels every now and then.

1 bronze fennel (*Foeniculum vulgare* 'Purpureum')

2 Cretan rock rose (*Cistus creticus*)

3 *Euphorbia myrsinites*

4 *Phlomis italica*

5 *Phlox douglasii*

6 rock rose (*Helianthemum*) 'Wisley Primrose'

7 sea kale (*Crambe maritima*)

8 *Stipa tenuissima*

9 *Tulipa sprengeri*

10 *Verbena bonariensis*

Prune Apple and Pear Trees

Most pruning of apple and pear trees is carried out
in winter, when plants are dormant, but those with
established restricted forms – fans, espaliers and
cordons – should be trimmed in late summer. Tackling
plants in late summer helps to control growth and
maintain an attractive shape, and encourages the
formation of buds that will carry fruit and flowers
next year. It's best to carry out work on a dry day as
the risk of infection by fungal diseases is much lower.
Using a pair of clean sharp secateurs, start by tackling
this season's shoots. Cut any that are 20cm (8in) long
and growing from a side branch back to one leaf. Any
new shoots growing from a main branch should be
reduced to three leaves.

FIVE GARDENS MADE FAMOUS FROM MYTHS, LEGENDS & RELIGIOUS BELIEFS

o **Garden of Eden** –
   appears in the book of
   Genesis in the Bible.

o **Garden of the
   Hesperides** – the
   goddess Hera's orchard
   in Greek mythology.

o **Garden of the gods** –
   described in the *Epic of
   Gilgamesh* from ancient
   Mesopotamia.

o **Hanging Gardens of
   Babylon** – one of the
   Seven Wonders of the
   Ancient World.

o **Xanadu** – Marco Polo
   described the gardens
   around Kublai Khan's
   legendary palace.

Sow Spring Onions

For an autumn treat, sow the seed of spring onions. Although spring onions (or salad onions as they are sometimes called) can be sown at any point from March until August, those started this month will provide pickings in October, when there are very few other salads around. There are lots of tangy varieties to try, which will be ready for harvesting in about eight weeks.

Growing spring onions in 30cm (12in) pots is easy. Fill with peat-free potting compost, firm and scatter seed thinly over the surface. Cover the seed with a 1cm (½in) layer of sieved compost. Place in a sunny spot and spray the surface with water. Thin out the seedlings to 2cm (¾in) apart when they're large enough to handle. Water regularly and cover with a cloche if frosts are forecast. Downy mildew disease can be a problem, so remove plants if you spot any white fungal growth.

THREE GREAT SPRING ONION VARIETIES TO TRY

1 'White Lisbon' - popular for its mild white stems and green tops.

2 'North Holland Blood Red' - has striking red stems and green tops.

3 'Summer Isle' - has a sweet mild flavour.

> **TOP TIP**
>
> If you fancy an early spring crop of salad onions, sow seed in September and protect seedlings over winter.

'The marigold observes the sun,

more than my subjects me have done.'

Charles I of England

Grow Rocket

Rocket is a leafy salad that really lives up to its name. Sow a pinch of seeds and they will blast into life, rewarding you with loads of piquant leaves within 21 days. Apart from being very easy to grow, the flavour of fresh leaves is on a different level to the contents of the pillow bags sold in shops.

SOWING IN THE GROUND AND IN POTS

Choose a sunny patch and make a shallow groove with the end of a garden cane. Then trickle seeds along the base, aiming to space them about 10cm (4in) apart. Cover the trench with soil and water. Another option is to raise rocket in 20cm (8in)-wide containers. Sow seed lightly across the surface, cover with lightly sieved compost and water.

THINNING OUT

Shoots usually appear within 7-14 days, depending on the variety and the weather. Make sure rocket plants have plenty of space to develop by thinning out seedlings when they are large enough to handle (about 4cm/1½in tall). Simply pull up with your fingers, leaving the remaining seedlings about 10cm (4in) apart.

MAINTAINING AND HARVESTING

Water regularly to prevent the soil or potting compost drying out, as this can lead to plants running to seed prematurely. Rocket is usually ready to harvest about four weeks after sowing and will provide pickings for a month or so. Take a few leaves as required from around the outside of plants, to ensure they produce plenty of fresh growth from the centre.

FOUR GREAT ROCKET VARIETIES TO TRY

Most seed companies stock a handful of different rocket varieties. Wild rocket is the one you'll recognize from supermarkets, with its frilly leaves and pungent taste. Other good ones include:

1 **'Discovery'** - has smooth-edged, elongated leaves.

2 **'Dragon's Tongue'** - boasts deeply lobed leaves that are marked with purple-red veins.

3 **'Sweet Oakleaf'** - bred in Britain to deal with cooler climates.

4 **'Wasabi'** - has scalloped-edged leaves that have the fiery taste of Japanese horseradish.

DID YOU KNOW ?

Despite what you might think, rocket doesn't get its common name because it's super speedy. It actually derives it from the Italian name for the salad veg, *rucola*, which itself comes from the plant's Latin name of *Eruca*. Elsewhere in the world, the French know the leaves as *rocquette* and Americans call it arugula. The Romans considered rocket a potent aphrodisiac, with the poet Virgil writing that it 'excites the sexual desires of drowsy people'.

Collect Seeds

Late summer until the end of autumn is the ideal time to gather the seeds from many plants that produce pods, capsules and seedheads. Among plants suitable for seed saving are hardy annuals, a host of perennials and some grasses. Collect seeds when ripe to ensure they'll germinate. This is usually evident by the seedheads turning from green to golden brown, or by capsules starting to crack open. Remove seeds from grasses by sliding them off with your fingers, and disperse the contents of the pods and capsules by shaking them into a bag; another option is to cut them off intact for extracting later.

Write the name of every plant you gather on the outside of collection bags. Empty the contents of bags onto sheets of white paper indoors. Remove debris, spread out the seeds and place them on a windowsill to dry for a few days. When they're ready, tip the seeds into envelopes, seal, label and place in an airtight container. Add a sachet of silica gel and keep in a cool dark place until sowing time in spring.

In most circumstances, only straight wild species (such as masterwort/ *Astrantia major*) will germinate true to type while cultivated varieties (like *Astrantia major* 'Large White') are normally propagated by another method, such as division. If you do save seeds from cultivated varieties, then be prepared for the seedlings to look different to their parent.

SAVE SEEDS FROM THESE…

HARDY ANNUALS

- common poppy (*Papaver rhoeas*)
- cornflower (*Centaurea cyanus*)
- larkspur (*Consolida ajacis*)
- love-in-a-mist (*Nigella damascena*)
- pot marigold (*Calendula officinalis*)

PERENNIALS

- common columbine (*Aquilegia vulgaris*)
- hollyhock (*Alcea rosea*)
- lady's mantle (*Alchemilla mollis*)
- masterwort (*Astrantia major*)
- regal lily (*Lilium regale*)

GRASSES

- foxtail barley (*Hordeum jubatum*)
- golden oats (*Stipa gigantea*)
- Mexican feather grass (*Stipa tenuissima*)
- purple love grass (*Eragrostis spectabilis*)
- tufted hair grass (*Deschampsia cespitosa*)

Take Semi-ripe Cuttings

One of the easiest ways of propagating a wide range of plants is to take cuttings in late summer. Nurserymen call these semi-ripe cuttings, because shoots are fairly firm or 'ripe' at the tail end of the growing season.

WHAT YOU NEED

Taking cuttings doesn't require fancy equipment. All you need is a pair of good-quality secateurs or a gardening knife as well as compost, labels and some small pots – 15cm (6in)-diameter ones are ideal. A heated propagator encourages cuttings to form roots, but it's not essential. As an alternative, place a clear freezer bag over pots and hold in place with an elastic band.

GATHERING MATERIAL

It's best to gather material early in the morning, rather than in the heat of the day. At this time, stems are full of water, which prevents them wilting quickly once cut. Always select healthy young shoots close to the top of plants, rather than older woodier growth. Steer clear of stems bearing flowers or buds, as they will drain energy from the cutting, thereby preventing roots forming.

Word buster:
Node

In plant science, nodes are the swellings on stems where buds, leaves and branches emerge. The spaces in between nodes are described as internodes.

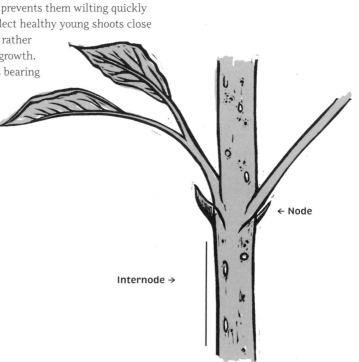

← Node

Internode →

1   Select healthy shoots with at least three sets of leaves, and remove them from the mother plant by cutting above a leaf joint. Place the shoots inside a bag with a little water in the bottom, shake and secure the top with an elastic band.

2   Take the material to a shady, sheltered spot, to prevent it from drying out quickly. Using a sharp gardening knife or secateurs, make a straight cut beneath a leaf joint. Aim to end up with a cutting that's 7.5-10cm (3-4in) in length.

3   Remove the leaves from the lower half to bottom third of each cutting (see illustration overleaf), using secateurs instead of your fingers, to avoid leaving behind jagged edges that can invite infection. Snip out the shoot tip if it is very soft and sappy.

4   Fill a clean, 15cm (6in) pot with specialist seed and cutting compost. Swipe your hand across the surface of the pot to roughly level the compost, and then tap to settle the contents. Firm down gently using the bottom of another pot.

5   Water the compost using a watering can with a rose or a hosepipe sprinkler, then allow to drain. Make three or four small holes around the outside of the pot with a pencil, then push a cutting into each hole, firming it into place with your fingers.

6   Stick a label in the pot and place in a heated propagator or under a sealed polythene bag cover. This will help the cuttings stay moist and speed up rooting.

↑ Semi-ripe cuttings should be about 7.5–10cm (3–4in) in length depending on the subject. Use a sharp knife to cut immediately below a node and then remove the lower leaves from the cutting.

NEXT STEPS

When the cuttings are well-rooted, take them out of the propagator or remove the polythene bag. You can check whether they are ready by looking for roots poking their way out of drainage holes or by giving them a gentle tug to see whether they are anchored. Allow to develop for a few weeks before breaking open the rootball and potting on individually into 7.5cm (3in) pots. Place in a light, frost-free place over winter and move into larger pots in early spring. Plant hardy species when established, and tender varieties after the last frost.

WHAT TO TAKE SEMI-RIPE CUTTINGS OF

SHRUBS

- barberry (*Berberis*)
- bottlebrush (*Callistemon*)
- California lilac (*Ceanothus*)
- common myrtle (*Myrtus communis*)
- escallonia

HERBS

- lavender (*Lavandula*)
- lemon verbena (*Aloysia citrodora*)
- rosemary (*Salvia rosmarinus*)
- sage (*Salvia*)
- thyme (*Thymus*)

TENDER PERENNIALS

- argyranthemum
- heliotrope (*Heliotropium*)
- busy Lizzie New Guinea Group (*Impatiens*)
- pelargonium
- verbena

CLIMBERS

- trumpet vine (*Campsis*)
- climbing hydrangea (*Hydrangea anomala subsp. petiolaris*)
- ivy (*Hedera*)
- passionflower (*Passiflora*)
- trachelospermum

TREES

- cercis
- holly (*Ilex*)
- *Magnolia grandiflora*
- yew (*Taxus*)

Sow Swiss Chard

This staple of Italian, French and Spanish cuisine is loved not only for its mild earthy flavour but also because it's one of the most attractive vegetables around, thanks to its architectural form, colourful stems and glossy leaves that look like they've been polished by hand. As a result, Swiss chard is pretty enough to be grown in borders as well as a dedicated veg patch. It'll do well in sun or partial shade, and likes rich, moisture-retentive soil.

Prior to sowing, prepare a seedbed (see page 97). Sow the seed in 2.5cm (1in)-deep furrows, spacing rows 35cm (14in) apart. Take a pinch of seed and scatter thinly along the furrow. Cover with soil and sprinkle gently with water. Seedlings should nose their way above the surface within 7-14 days. Once they are large enough to handle, thin them out to 30cm (12in) apart. Keep well-watered, especially during dry spells, and feed every couple of weeks with a high-nitrogen fertilizer. Leaves will be ready for picking in about 12 weeks. Take what you need from around the outside, cutting off with a sharp knife. Regular picking will ensure lots of fresh leaves are produced from the centre of the plant.

FIVE CRACKING CHARD VARIETIES TO TRY

1 **'Bright Lights'** - a blend of red, white, orange, yellow and pink stems.

2 **'Fordhook Giant'** - thigh-high, white stems topped by large green leaves.

3 **'Lucullus'** - large, glossy green leaves and contrasting white stems.

4 **'Orange Fantasia'** - neon-orange stems and leaf veins.

5 **'Peppermint'** - glossy, dark green leaves and two-tone, pink and white stems.

WHO AM I?

Poor old Swiss chard has a bit of an identity crisis. As well as the common name referred to here, the plant is known by many other names around the world. For example, silver beet, perpetual spinach, Sicilian beet, crab beet, seakale beet, strawberry spinach, beet spinach and leaf beet are just some of the names in regular use.

HEALTH BENEFITS OF SWISS CHARD

Swiss chard is highly nutritious. It's low in calories and a good source of calcium, iron, magnesium and potassium, along with vitamins A, C and K.

Pest and Disease Watch: Rosemary Beetle

This ladybird-sized, oval insect, marked by metallic-green and purple stripes, has a voracious appetite for the leaves of rosemary (*Salvia rosmarinus*), lavender (*Lavandula*), sage (*Salvia*) and thyme (*Thymus*). Adult beetles lay their eggs on plants, which hatch into larvae that also feed on plants before heading to the soil beneath vulnerable plants to pupate. Fortunately, this insect sticks out like a sore thumb, so keep a close eye on plants and pick them off before they have the chance to strip stems of foliage.

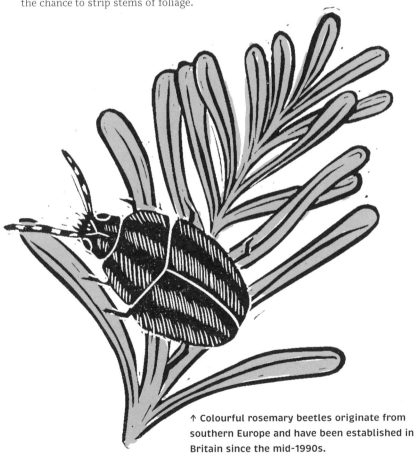

↑ Colourful rosemary beetles originate from southern Europe and have been established in Britain since the mid-1990s.

'September days are here,

With summer's best of weather,

And autumn's best of cheer'

(Helen Hunt Jackson, *September*)

THE MONTH AT A GLANCE

- Cut back pelargoniums to 10cm (4in) and store in a frost-free place over winter.
- Prune tatty perennials (see Cut Back Perennials, page 176).
- Tie in new shoots of climbers and wall shrubs, to prevent damage in windy weather.
- Remove summer bedding plants that have gone past their best.
- Plant spring-flowering bulbs (see page 177).
- Sow hardy annual seeds (page 186).
- Pick apples when fruit easily twists off branches.
- Watch out for brown rot on plums.
- Plant spring cabbages (see Grow Spring Cabbages, page 174).
- Cut back and store chilli pepper plants (see Overwinter Chilli Peppers, page 182).
- Cut back asparagus stems when the foliage starts to turn yellow.
- Plant seed potatoes for Christmas (see Grow Some Festive Potatoes, page 182).
- Harvest and store fruit and vegetables (see Store Fruit & Vegetables, page 184).
- Treat moss, relieve compaction and feed lawns (see Give Lawns a Pick-Me-Up, page 172).
- Naturalize bulbs in lawns (see page 178).
- Plant up containers for winter interest (see Create a Winter Container, page 170).
- Compost garden waste (see Start a Compost Bin, page 168).
- Scrub off shade paint or remove shade netting from inside greenhouses.
- Close greenhouse doors in mid-afternoon, to trap in warmth and keep plants snug overnight.
- Tackle tortrix moths (see Pest and Disease Watch: Tortrix Moth, page 187).
- Move houseplants back inside if they spent summer outdoors (see Moving Houseplants Back Indoors, page 141).

September

We might be lucky enough to experience an Indian summer but, as far as meteorologists are concerned, we are now in autumn. It might sound a bit counterintuitive to be thinking ahead to spring at this time, but this is when garden centres, DIY stores and nurseries take the wraps off their early-flowering bulbs such as daffodils and crocus. Snap these up as soon as possible, to ensure you get what you want. This can be a busy month with edibles needing harvesting and summer-worn lawns begging for a pick-me-up.

Start a Compost Bin

Gardens generate lots of unwanted waste, from shrub prunings to spent vegetable plants, and from grass clippings to flowerheads. Rather than consigning this stuff to the rubbish bin, recycle it by placing in a compost bin, turning it into an open, nutrient-rich material that can be used for mulching or improving soil.

WHAT TYPE OF BIN?

Purpose-built, square, wooden bins are widely available and can hold considerable amounts of waste. Alternatively, erect a home-made bin from wooden pallets. A further option is to choose a bin that comes with a fitted lid and a hatch at the base, to access material; Dalek-shaped plastic models are compact enough to be pushed into a corner, while wooden beehive types will sit perfectly in a bed or border.

A three-bay composting system is best: one bin for filling; one for the waste while it composts; and the third for ready use. Site the bin or bins on a flat spot, ideally on soil or grass, to improve drainage and provide access for worms.

TYPES OF WASTE

The type of material put into a compost heap is split into two main groups: greens and browns. Soft material that rots down quickly falls into the green camp, adding nitrogen and moisture to the mix. Browns comprise drier materials, rich in carbon, and they provide fibre and so give the compost its structure. On their own, greens produce a smelly sludge, so add equal amounts of browns to your mix.

WHAT TO COMPOST

- annual weeds
- broken eggshells
- coffee grounds
- dried leaves
- lawn clippings
- plant trimmings
- shredded newspaper
- spent flowerheads
- tea leaves
- vegetable peelings

WHAT TO AVOID WHEN COMPOSTING

- animal waste
- bread
- cat litter
- cooked food
- diseased plant material
- fish
- fresh perennial weeds
- glossy paper
- human waste
- meat

» HOW TO MAKE GARDEN COMPOST «

1   Spread a little well-rotted manure across the bottom of the bin to encourage worm activity.

2   Start to add garden waste, making sure that for every bucket of nitrogen-rich green material you add an equal amount of carbon-rich brown material.

3   If the bin doesn't have a lid, place a waterproof cover on top to prevent the contents getting too soggy.

4   Large amounts of one material can be slow to rot, so mix the contents regularly with a garden fork.

5   In hot sunny spells, the contents of bins can dry out. Sprinkle with water occasionally, to prevent a check to composting.

6   Continue to add waste to the bin. The compost is ready when the material at the bottom is sweet-smelling, brown and crumbly.

WHAT TO DO WITH YOUR COMPOST

Garden compost and leafmould (see page 214) make an ideal mulch, when spread in a 5cm (2in) layer over soil between late winter and early spring. Leave a gap around plant stems, to prevent softening leading to rotting. It also makes a good soil conditioner when dug into the ground, helping to improve structure, workability and moisture retention.

Another option is to use garden compost to make your own potting mix using equal parts garden compost, leafmould and topsoil. This mix is great for trees, shrubs and perennials, but is too bulky for seeds and could contain pathogens, so don't use for raising sensitive seedlings.

PROJECT: Create a Winter Container

Add a pop of colour to your winter patio by planting up a container. There are loads of seasonal bedding plants currently available in garden centres that will take cold weather in their stride. Some will flower constantly until early spring, while others give more of a stop-start performance. You can create a container arrangement using just bedding plants, but it's more effective to combine them with perennials, shrubs, conifers and grasses to produce a display that provides colour, texture, structure and movement.

YOU WILL NEED

- A selection of plants   ∘   Peat-free, multipurpose potting compost
- 30-45cm (12-18in)-wide container   ∘   Watering can

TRY THESE PLANTS

- winter-flowering pansies (*Viola × wittrockiana*)
- ornamental cabbages
- polyanthus (*Primula*)
- primroses (*Primula vulgaris*)
- bedding cyclamen
- dogwood (*Cornus sanguinea* WINTER FLAME)
- Mexican feather grass (*Stipa tenuissima*)
- black dragon grass (*Ophiopogon planiscapus* 'Nigrescens')

HOW TO PLANT A CONTAINER

1 Soak the plants (still in their pots) in a bucket of water for at least an hour before planting. Leave to drain.

2 Tip some peat-free, multipurpose potting compost into the container

3 Remove the largest plant from its plastic pot and place in the compost - the surface of the rootball should sit about 5cm (2in) beneath the top of the pot.

4 Add more plants, using compost to raise the level for those in smaller pots.

5 Pack the plants in tightly, filling any gaps with compost and water thoroughly.

Lasagne Planting

If you only have room for one container, then try lasagne planting, so named because three different bulbs are planted in layers, like the famous Italian dish. Rather than growing varieties that bloom at the same time, the idea is to choose those that will provide a succession of colour over a long period of time. Dwarf Iris reticulata, daffodil (Narcissus) 'Tête-à-Tête' and *Tulipa* 'Angélique' make a great combination. Start by putting a layer of potting compost into a 30cm (12in) container and add the tulips. These should be about 20cm (8in) beneath the rim of the pot and can be packed in quite closely, provided they don't touch. Cover with 5cm (2in) of compost, then add the daffodils. Cover as before, then finish with a layer of irises. Top up with compost and water. In late winter, the display will begin with the iris, followed by the daffodils and end with the tulips in May.

Reuse Grow-Bags

Don't get rid of the compost from grow-bags once your summer crops have gone over. Although all the nutrients will have been depleted, the compost will be fine for growing a quick crop of salad leaves. Prepare the bag by cutting out a generous rectangular panel, break up the compost if it is compacted and comb through to remove as many of the previous occupants' roots as possible. Add some fresh compost to fill up the bag and gently spread out the material until even with your fingers, leaving a level finish. Either sow the seed in short rows across the width of the bag or in longer rows along its length.

THE BINOMIAL SYSTEM OF NOMENCLATURE

We have pioneering Swedish botanist Carl Linnaeus to thank for the binomial system of nomenclature that is used to identify plants. Back in 1753, he gave plants a generic name (or genus) and a specific name (or species). For example, under the system he invented, which is still in use today, the common oak tree became *Quercus* (genus) *robur* (species). In the 20th century, the system was updated to include a cultivar name, given to plants that have been produced in cultivation – this name is enclosed within single quotation marks, as in *Quercus robur* 'Koster'.

Give Lawns a Pick-Me-Up

A cocktail of drought, downpours and scorching heat, along with heavy foot traffic over summer, can leave lawns in an awful shape by early autumn. Fortunately, this is the perfect time to carry out some lawn maintenance. Apart from reviving its good looks, giving your patch of turf some one-to-one attention will help to prepare it for winter.

TREAT MOSS

If you have a problem with moss, eliminate it with a non-chemical moss remover, such as MO Bacter. Unlike chemical moss killers, the granules feed grass but overfeed moss, thereby helping to kill it. Apart from being better for the environment, the product doesn't turn the moss an unsightly black colour, and there's no need to rake it out as the moss will simply break down naturally.

RELIEVE COMPACTION

Improve parts of the lawn subjected to heavy foot traffic. In these areas, soil particles are pressed tightly together, reducing the amount of air and moisture the ground can hold. Unfortunately, compaction leads to weak growth, poor drainage and moss. Push a fork into the ground as deeply as you can, wiggle it about and repeat every 10cm (4in) across the problem patch. Brush some ready-made topdressing (a mixture of loam and sand) into the holes.

FEEDING LAWNS

Summer rain can wash a lot of nutrients out of the soil beneath lawns, leaving grass looking yellow and generally lacking vigour. Perk lawns up by giving them a good feed. Fertilizers suitable for applying in autumn are high in phosphates and potash, which encourage strong roots and healthy leaves and toughen up grass in preparation for the colder weather to come. Either distribute by hand or use a wheeled spreader (see page 72).

CUTTING ADVICE

Lawns need frequent cutting during spring and summer, but grass will still require the occasional trim in autumn, especially if the weather is mild. Raise the cutting height of the mower blades so you don't run the risk of scalping the surface - exposing soil to the elements allows frost to penetrate, resulting in damage to the roots of grass over winter. A cutting height of 5-7cm (2-2½in) is an ideal height for most family lawns in the autumn.

Lawn Alternatives

Lawns are desirable features, but they do require a lot of attention if you want to keep them in good condition. If maintaining one is starting to drive you up the wall, there are several low-maintenance alternatives to consider.

CHAMOMILE LAWNS

These are suitable for areas that receive light foot traffic. To establish one, start by preparing a seedbed (see page 97) and then place an order for some plugs or larger plants of a non-flowering form of chamomile, such as *Chamaemelum nobile* 'Treneague'. Plant at 10-25cm (4-10in) intervals, depending on their size. Water and keep the site weed-free until established. Do not walk on the lawn for 12 weeks after planting, and allow only light traffic for its first year.

TAPESTRY LAWNS

This type of lawn consists of several flowering groundcover plants set closely together, to prevent weeds from growing. *Sagina subulata*, chamomile (*Chamaemelum nobile* 'Treneague'), creeping thyme (*Thymus pseudolanuginosus*), New Zealand bur (*Acaena microphylla*) and similar species that can tolerate some footfall will cope admirably.

Arrange individual species 15cm (6in) apart, watering regularly for the first couple of years. Once established, the surface will need mowing only three or five times a year.

SEDUM LAWNS

Areas that get little or no foot traffic are suitable for a sedum lawn. Supplied in rolls, matting is impregnated with a blend of succulents such as *Sedum album* and *Sedum sexangulare*. Apart from providing a floral display from spring until autumn, sedum lawns don't require any watering, deadheading or mowing.

Trivia time

There might not be any plants named after Boris Johnson, Tony Blair or Harold Wilson, but there are several that honour other British prime ministers. *Colchicum* 'Disraeli' is a meadow saffron dubbed after 19th-century Conservative prime minister Benjamin Disraeli, while *Clematis* 'W E Gladstone' was chosen to celebrate William Ewart Gladstone, who was Liberal prime minster four times in the late 1800s. *Narcissus* 'Sir Winston Churchill' is a multiheaded daffodil with scented flowers, which was named after the famous Second World War leader.

Cut Back Perennials

Restore a sense of order to borders by cutting back perennials that have finished flowering. Many plants benefit from being chopped to ground level as their spent stems look unsightly and they can damage the crown of the plant when pounded by the wind over winter. However, don't be too hasty and prune everything. Some plants have seedheads that add sculptural detail when there's little else of interest around, along with providing food for hungry birds.

PRUNE THESE PERENNIALS

- *Astrantia* 'Roma'
- *Crambe cordifolia*
- *Crocosmia* × *crocosmiiflora* 'Emily McKenzie'
- *Euphorbia griffithii* 'Fireglow'
- *Filipendula ulmaria*

LEAVE THESE PERENNIALS

- *Calamagrostis* × *acutiflora* 'Karl Foerster'
- *Eryngium giganteum* 'Silver Ghost'
- *Hylotelephium spectabile*
- *Pennisetum alopecuroides*
- *Rudbeckia fulgida* var. *sullivantii* 'Goldsturm'

**Word buster:
Sport**

A genetic mutation that results in part of a plant changing appearance. Sparked by insect damage, cold weather or other reasons, a genetic mutation can occur in the leaves, stems, fruit or flowers of any plant. Many popular garden plants have arisen from sports, which are removed from the parent plant and propagated at nurseries. One example is variegated holly (*Ilex*) 'Golden van Tol', a sport of plain green holly 'J C van Tol'.

↓ The seedheads of many perennials will provide interest into winter, but those belonging to some perennials will collapse. Remove stems by cutting them off close to ground level, just above the crown.

Prairie-style Planting

During the early 2000s, traditional herbaceous borders were given a run for their money when leading garden designers started to create naturalistic displays inspired by the grasslands of the American Midwest. Dubbed 'prairie planting', the style originally featured late-flowering perennials and grasses from North America, which were planted in large swathes to provide height, texture and movement. In general, prairie-style plantings should contain two-thirds perennials to one-third grasses.

FIVE PERENNIALS FOR PRAIRIE-STYLE PLANTING

1 *Coreopsis grandiflora* 'Early Sunrise'

2 *Echinacea purpurea* 'Magnus'

3 *Helenium* 'Moerheim Beauty'

4 *Rudbeckia triloba* 'Prairie Glow'

5 *Veronicastrum virginicum*

FIVE GREAT GRASSES

1 *Calamagrostis* x *acutiflora* 'Karl Foerster'

2 *Deschampsia cespitosa* 'Goldtau'

3 *Molinia caerulea* subsp. *arundinacea* 'Transparent'

4 *Panicum virgatum*

5 *Stipa tenuissima*

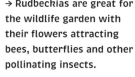

→ Rudbeckias are great for the wildlife garden with their flowers attracting bees, butterflies and other pollinating insects.

Plant Spring-flowering Bulbs

Spring-flowering bulbs are essential for adding early colour to beds, borders, containers, lawns and other parts of the garden. Ornamental onions (*Allium*), crocuses, daffodils (*Narcissus*), dwarf irises, fritillaries (*Fritillaria*), grape hyacinths (*Muscari*), winter aconites (*Eranthis hyemalish*) and the rest are available to buy from August, but they fare best if set in soil in September or October, when the soil is still warm yet moist after some autumn rain.

When buying bulbs, reject any that are mouldy, damaged, shrivelled or feel squishy if you give them a gentle squeeze. Bulbs come in varying sizes with larger ones producing better flowers. You'll have to take what's available in shops but select 'top size' bulbs if ordering from online specialists.

As a general rule, bulbs need to be planted at a depth two or three times their length. A trowel is fine for digging holes if you've got only a handful, while a long-handled bulb planter makes light work of larger numbers. If your soil is on the heavy side, add some sharp grit to the base of the hole to improve drainage.

Trivia time

In the Harry Potter world of wizarding, characters are equipped with wands made from different woody plants. These are some of the most important ones:

- **Albus Dumbledore**
  – elder (*Sambucus*)
- **Draco Malfoy**
  – hawthorn (*Crataegus*)
- **Harry Potter**
  – holly (*Ilex*)
- **Hermione Granger**
  – vine (*Vitis*)
- **Lord Voldemort**
  – yew (*Taxus*)
- **Ron Weasley**
  – willow (*Salix*)
- **Rubeus Hagrid**
  – oak (*Quercus*)

TOP TIP

Compact bulbs are perfect in containers filled with peat-free potting compost. After planting, outwit foraging squirrels by placing a sheet of chicken wire over the top, folding down the sides to keep it in place. Remove once shoots appear.

Naturalize Bulbs in Lawns

A great way of displaying bulbs is to naturalize them in long or short grass. It's best to choose early-flowering varieties because, once the flowers go over, plants will need to be left to die back naturally before mowing can start in earnest. For a natural-looking display, drop a handful of bulbs from waist height and plant them where they land. Repeat the process in several areas.

Use a long-handled planter to set large bulbs in the lawn. Remove a core of soil, drop in a bulb and cover with soil. Remember to pop the cap of turf back on top.

↓ Place the long-handled planter over the spot where you want to plant a bulb and push downward, using your weight on the treaded edge foot grip. Give it a slight twist and pull upward to remove a core of soil.

FIVE GREAT SPRING-FLOWERING BULBS TO TRY

1 *Crocus tommasinianus* **'Barr's Purple'** - during February and March, this diminutive gem adds a splash of pink-purple with its cup-shaped blooms.

2 **daffodil (*Narcissus*) 'February Gold'** - a cracking bulb that bears golden flowers on 30cm (12in) stems in February and March.

3 **dog's tooth violet (*Erythronium dens-canis*)** - in mid- to late spring, slender stems carry nodding violet flowers with swept-back petals above clumps of showy, mottled leaves.

4 **hyacinth (*Hyacinthus orientalis*) 'Purple Sensation'** - sturdy stems up to 20cm (8in) in height are packed with heavily perfumed, tubular, pink-purple flowers in March and April.

5 **snake's head fritillary (*Fritillaria meleagris*)** - a compact beauty with nodding, lantern-like flowers chequered with pink, purple and white markings.

'When people will not weed their own minds, they are apt to be overrun by nettles.'

Horace Walpole

A LITTLE BIT ABOUT DAFFODILS

Known botanically as *Narcissus*, daffodils largely come from Spain, Italy and Portugal, along with a few other European countries. The Lent lily (*Narcissus pseudonarcissus*) is native to the UK and is believed to be the parent of the Tenby daffodil (*N. obvallaris*), which thrives in parts of south Wales. Breeding work on these wild plants, especially during a boom in the 1950s, has led to a staggering number of different varieties – the Royal Horticultural Society's *Plant Finder* guide lists over 3,000 available in the UK, with more being introduced each year. There is great diversity among the tribe. Ranging in height between 10cm (4in) to almost 60cm (24in), plants are topped by single or double flowers that consist of a trumpet or cup (technically, a corona) and a cluster of outer petals (technically, tepals) known collectively as the perianth. Most flowers are yellow and white, but some have red, orange or pink coronas, creating a two-tone effect.

Grow Spring Cabbages

Spring can be a lean time in the veg patch, so ensure there are pickings by planting spring cabbages. Young plants are readily available from garden centres and online specialists in late summer and early autumn. Cabbages like a sunny spot with fertile, well-drained and fairly firm soil - tamp down recently cultivated soil with the back of a rake. Like all brassicas, cabbages do best in neutral to alkaline ground. If you have acidic soil, sprinkle some garden lime over the surface, a month or so before planting out. This will reduce the risk of clubroot, a fungal disease that is more prevalent in acidic soil, causing stunted growth and wilting.

Set cabbage plants 45cm (18in) apart, to ensure they have room to form decent-sized heads. Keep the soil free of weeds, and water during dry spells. In early spring, give cabbages a pick-me-up by drenching the soil around them with liquid feed or by scattering poultry manure pellets around them.

Cabbages will be ready for harvesting in April or May. Either pull up entire plants, roots and all, or cut the heads off with a sharp knife close to ground level - a clever trick is to score the top of the stump with a 1cm (½in)-deep cross, to encourage mini-cabbages to form from the incision.

FOUR TASTY SPRING CABBAGE VARIETIES TO TRY

1 **'April'** - forming upright, compact heads this is ideal where space is tight as plants can be spaced as close as 30cm (12in) apart.

2 **'Duncan'** - forms dense pointed heads up to 450g (1lb) in weight with crisp, sweet and nutty-flavoured leaves.

3 **'Durham Early'** - its dark green, firm, conical heads are super tasty with a crunchy texture.

4 **'Spring Hero'** - has compact round heads, which are super-sweet.

Grow Some Festive Potatoes

It's normal for gardeners to plant potatoes in spring for harvesting in summer, but you can plant tubers of some varieties in early autumn, for spuds that will be ready for unearthing during the festive season. 'Charlotte', 'Maris Peer' and 'Nicola' are among the varieties that are generally available for this purpose. As it's too cold to plant them in the ground, raise in 40cm (16in)-wide pots. Add a 10cm (4in) layer of multipurpose potting compost, place three tubers on the surface (there's no need to chit), cover with a 5cm (2in) layer of compost and add three more tubers. Cover again and water. Stow the pot away in an unheated greenhouse, porch or cool conservatory.

As the shoots grow, add more compost, stopping when you have almost filled the pot. Make sure you keep the compost damp, but don't overwater.

Overwinter Chilli Peppers

Most people consign chilli pepper plants to the compost heap once the last of the fruit has been picked, but it is possible to keep container-grown plants going from one season to the next. Prepare plants by removing all the fruit and foliage and then prune the stems down to about 15cm (6in), leaving a compact stubby framework. Move the plant to a frost-free place, such as a greenhouse, front porch or windowsill, and aim to keep it at a temperature of 5-12°C (41-54°F). Water occasionally, to prevent the compost from drying out completely. As light levels and temperatures pick up in spring, leaves should appear and you can water more regularly. Overwintered chilli plants usually flower and fruit earlier than those started from seed in spring.

↓ To overwinter chilli plants, first remove the fruit and then reduce the length of all stems. It's important not to not prune stems too hard as the plant may not recover.

Store Fruit & Vegetables

The arrival of cooler nights and the threat of an early frost in some parts of the country make it important to harvest crops before time runs out. Don't worry, you don't need to eat everything immediately. Some crops can be stored after picking, to provide food over the next few months - often well into winter.

» MAKE AN ONION ROPE «

A traditional onion rope looks good and allows air to circulate around bulbs, reducing the risk of fungal diseases.

1 Let the bulbs dry thoroughly, then cut a 60cm (24in) length of twine.

2 Gather three bulbs together and tie a knot above their necks. Then wind the foliage around the twine.

3 Add more bulbs, letting them rest on those below and winding the foliage upward.

4 When you run out of space, tie a firm knot around the onions at the top.

5 Use the tops of the foliage to form a loop and hang the onion rope in a cool dry place.

6 Cut the bulbs from the rope, as and when needed.

APPLES AND PEARS

Late-ripening apples, along with pears, will keep for many months if stored correctly. Harvest apples when they come away from the tree with a gentle twist, and pears when they are still hard, green and under-ripe - eject any with damaged skin or visible signs of rotting. Wrap apples individually in tissue paper or sheets of newspaper and place in a single layer in wooden trays. Pears can be placed in trays without wrapping, but ensure that individual fruits are not touching. Store in a cool, frost-free garage or shed.

CURING PUMPKINS AND SQUASH

Fresh pumpkins and squash will last for just a few weeks after harvesting but, if 'cured' first, can be stored for up to six months. Harvest the fruit when ripe, leaving a 10cm (4in) stub of stem. Place the fruit in a single layer in a sunny spot, such as a bench inside a greenhouse or a light porch, for about two weeks to allow the skin to harden - this will prevent the flesh from drying out. Set the cured fruit in a cool, dry, airy and frost-free place - ideally raise them up on wire racks, cushioned with newspaper, to allow air to circulate underneath.

CHILLI PEPPER STRING

Originating from South America as a way of storing a glut of chilli peppers for using at a later date, a ristra is a simple string of dried fruit that can be hung in a prominent place in the kitchen. Pick fruit before the first frosts, leaving a good portion of the green stem attached. Take a length of fishing line and tie a knot on one end, and then thread the other end through the eye of a large needle. Next, thread the needle through the stem of each pepper, arranging them in a circular pattern on the line. When complete, hang the ristra in a light airy spot indoors to dry.

> ### Word buster:
> ### Bletting
>
> Derived from the French *poire blette*, meaning 'over-ripe pear', bletting is the process of allowing the fruit of some trees to soften and sweeten once picked. For example, ripe medlar fruit is hard and inedible. Once picked it needs to be stored in a cool dry place for about three weeks until the flesh is mushy and appears dark brown.

Sow Hardy Annuals

The quickest way to add a splash of colour to gardens is to sow seeds of hardy annuals. These can be sown directly into the soil now to bloom by the end of next spring. Preferring a sunny spot and well-drained soil, the seeds of individual varieties are perfect for filling gaps between permanent plants in beds and borders. Another option is to brighten up a larger empty patch of soil with hardy annuals. To do this, start by preparing the ground by gently forking over and then raking the surface to a fine even finish. Mark out a paisley-style pattern on the surface, using sand. Sprinkle seeds from a different flower in each section, using smaller varieties at the edges and larger plants in the middle or toward the back. Rake lightly to cover and water.

After germination, thin out the seedlings to 2.5cm (1in) apart, to prevent overcrowding. Repeat the thinning process in a few weeks' time, leaving 15cm (6in) between the remaining plants.

FIVE GREAT HARDY ANNUALS TO SOW NOW

1 corn cockle (*Agrostemma*)

2 godetia (*Clarkia*)

3 honeywort (*Cerinthe*)

4 love-in-a-mist (*Nigella*)

5 pot marigold (*Calendula*)

OFFICIAL FLOWERS OF US STATES

Each of the 50 states that makes up the United States of America has its own official flower. Here are ten that grow wild there and are also popular garden plants in the UK:

- **Alabama** – Camellia japonica
- **Arkansas** – apple (*Malus domestica*) blossom
- **California** – California poppy (*Eschscholzia californica*)
- **Connecticut** – mountain laurel (*Kalmia latifolia*)
- **Indiana** – peony (*Paeonia*)
- **Kansas** – sunflower (*Helianthus annuus*)
- **Maryland** – black-eyed Susan (*Rudbeckia hirta*)
- **New Hampshire** – lilac (*Syringa vulgaris*)
- **New Mexico** – yucca
- **Oregon** – Oregon grape (*Mahonia aquifolium*)

Pest and Disease Watch: Tortrix moth

These tiny brown moths lay their eggs on a wide range of plants. The eggs hatch into small, slim, green caterpillars that bind or curl leaves together with silken threads so they can feed safely on the leaf from the inside. In order to prevent damage to foliage, check plants regularly, open up any leaves that are stuck together and squish the caterpillar inside.

↓ Check plants regularly for tortrix moth caterpillars, which are most active between April and September on outdoor plants.

'Nature now spreads around in dreary hue

A pall to cover all that summer knew.'

(John Clare, *The Shepherd's Calendar – October*)

THE MONTH AT A GLANCE

- Plant climbers (see Grow Climbers, page 200).
- Install training wires for climbers (see How to Install Training Wires on a Fence, page 197).
- Use tree stakes and netting to make a temporary shelter to protect newly planted evergreens against windscorch (see Staking Trees, page 194).
- Remove unwanted self-seeded perennials before they have a chance to establish.
- Rake up fallen rose leaves, to prevent the spread of blackspot disease.
- Control fungal leaf spots on winter-flowering pansies (*Viola × wittrockiana*), by picking off infected leaves.
- Plant blackberries (see Blackberries in Pots, page 206).
- Cut off bunches of green tomatoes from plants and ripen indoors.
- Plant blueberries in pots or the ground (see Plant Blueberries, page 207).
- Sow green manure seeds (see Sow Green Manure, page 190).
- Plant cloves of garlic (see Get Going with Garlic, page 204).
- Sow hardy varieties of pea for harvesting in late spring (see Start Peas from Seed, page 89).
- Sow broad bean seeds (see Sow Broad Beans, page 202).
- Dig the soil (see Dig the Soil, page 190).
- Lay lawns with turf (see Lay a Lawn, page 192).
- Lift and divide aquatic perennials (see Improve your pond, page 78).
- Make hibernating habitats for wildlife (see Make a Home for Wildlife, page 196).
- Remove fading leaves from greenhouse plants before they drop and trigger fungal diseases (see Pest and Disease Watch: Grey Mould, page 38).
- Check greenhouse heaters are working before frosts arrive.

October

What a difference a few short weeks can make. The
weather is noticeably cooler, and when the clocks
go back toward the end of the month we'll be left
with shorter days. Frosts are a definite possibility
in some parts of the country, yet it's a lovely month
to spend time in the garden - the air smells musty
but pleasant, while the leaves of trees and shrubs
will be starting to take on hues of yellow, orange
and red. Their colours are accentuated on days
when they are illuminated by the low autumn sun.

Sow Green Manure

Mention manure and most people will think of the pungent, crumbly, brown stuff that can be bought in bags from a stable. However, there's another type. Green manures are fast-growing, nutrient-rich crops that are ideal for sowing on bare soil, whether it's an allotment plot or veg patch. They can be sown in rows, or scattered across the soil and raked into the surface. Green manures are best left to grow for two or three months before being dug into the ground. Apart from giving the soil a nutritional boost, their fibrous root systems will improve soil structure and the carpet of greenery will prevent weeds from growing. Grazing rye (*Secale cereale*), winter tares (*Vicia sativa*) and winter field bean (*Vicia faba*) are among the green manures suitable for sowing in mid-autumn.

> **TOP TIP**
>
> Avoid accidents by never digging when the soil is frozen or waterlogged, and always wear boots or wellies with reinforced toecaps.

Dig the Soil

If you have an allotment plot or veg patch, or plan to start a new lawn or border in spring, then now is the time to prepare the soil. Digging allows frost to break down heavy clods, making it perfect for sowing and planting, while exposing soilborne pests, such as wireworms, to hungry birds. There are three main ways of cultivating the ground: simple, single and double digging.

THE NO-DIG METHOD

No-dig gardening is a method long practised by organic vegetable growers but is suitable for those with back problems or who are less fit, along with folk who don't have enough free time to dig their plots. Rather than turn over the ground on an annual basis, exponents of no-dig start by covering the surface with a 10-15cm (4-6in)-deep layer of garden compost or fully rotted manure. Seeds or plants are then set directly into this surface layer, preventing the structure of the soil and organisms underneath from being disturbed. From then on, a 5cm (2in) top up of organic matter is spread over the ground each autumn.

SIMPLE DIGGING

Simple digging is suitable when working around established plants in beds and borders. All you need to do is lift a clod with your spade, turn it over and drop it back in the ground before chopping it up with the spade. It's easier to turn over heavy or stony soil with a fork.

SINGLE DIGGING

This is perfect for allotment plots and patches of soil that are in regular cultivation, and it involves excavating a trench to the depth of the spade's blade (a measurement known as a 'spit') and transporting the soil in a wheelbarrow to the other end of the area to be cultivated. Dig out another trench parallel to the first one and drop the soil into this. Carry on in this way until you reach the end of the plot, filling the final trench with the soil you moved earlier.

DOUBLE DIGGING

You will find this harder work than other methods, as it requires cultivating soil to the depth of two 'spits'; it is best used on ground that hasn't been cultivated for some time. Start by digging out a trench to the depth of the spade's blade and moving the soil to the other end of the area (as with single digging, see left). Use a fork to break up the soil in the base, pushing the prongs as deep as possible into the ground. Continue like this to the end. Then dig a second trench parallel to the first, dropping the soil into the first one and forking over the base. Continue like this until the whole area is dug; use the soil from the first trench to fill the last one.

↓ Single digging is ideal on regular shaped patches of ground, where it's important that the soil has a consistent and even texture.

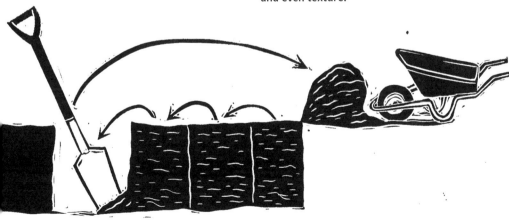

PROJECT: Lay a Lawn

The quickest and easiest way of creating a new lawn is by laying rolls of turf in autumn or spring. The weather tends to be cool and damp in these seasons, allowing roots to establish readily. During hot and cold weather, new lawns are placed under stress and are unlikely to thrive.

Always order turf from a reputable supplier, to ensure it is weed-, disease- and pest-free. A standard roll measures 1.64 × 0.61m (5ft 4in × 24in) and covers an area of 1 sq. m (10¾ sq. ft), so work out how many you need and order an extra one or two in case of accidents. When the turf is delivered, store it in a shady spot and sprinkle with water, to prevent it from drying out. As a rule, it's best to lay turf within two days of delivery - if laying is delayed, open the rolls to stop the grass yellowing.

YOU WILL NEED

∘ Turf ∘ Spade ∘ Fork ∘ Rake ∘ Knife ∘ Scaffolding boards
∘ Half-moon tool ∘ Length of hosepipe ∘ Ready-made topsoil
∘ Broom ∘ Hosepipe and sprinkler head

HOW TO DO IT

1 Prepare the ground by skimming off old grass with a spade and removing weeds and large stones. Fork over, roughly level by raking and firm by walking up and down. Continue raking until the surface is even and the texture like coarse breadcrumbs.

2 Lay your first row of turfs along a straight edge, carefully unwinding to avoid tearing. Butt every piece up tight against the previous one until the first row is complete, and then give each one a tap with the back of the rake to ensure it makes good contact with the soil Finish the end of the row with a half-size piece of turf.

3 Lay the next and subsequent rows by staggering the pieces of turf in a running bond brickwork pattern, making sure they fit snugly. Avoid damaging the turf by working from planks of wood laid along the previous row.

4 Unless you are laying a square lawn, edges will need trimming. Curved sides are easily created using a half-moon tool and a length of hosepipe as a cutting guide.

5 Finish by brushing a sandy topsoil mix into the cracks with a broom, and water well.

↓ It's important to avoid walking on freshly
laid turf. Use scaffolding planks to fetch new
pieces for laying, which will help to distribute
your weight and prevent damage.

How to Plant a Tree

Autumn is the traditional time for planting all sorts of trees - the soil is still warm from summer and damp from recent rain, allowing plants to form a mass of roots in the ground.

CONTAINER-GROWN TREES

Planting container-grown trees is easy. Dig a round hole that's twice the diameter of the container and the same depth. Spike the sides and bottom of the hole with a fork, to allow the roots to penetrate. Place the tree in the centre and fill gaps with soil, firming as you go to remove air pockets. In the past, it was recommended that well-rotted manure or garden compost should be placed in the bottom of the hole. However, this should be avoided because trees will sink as the material rots. Water and mulch with a 5cm (2in) layer of well-rotted manure, garden compost or leafmould.

BARE-ROOT TREES

Bare-root specimens need planting at the same depth as they were growing before being lifted from the ground - there should be an obvious 'tide mark' of soil on the trunk. Dig a hole that's twice the diameter of the root system and deep enough so the mark on the trunk lines up with the soil surface. It's possible to do this by eye but, to make sure, put the tree in position and lay a garden cane across the hole. If the cane does not line up with the mark, add or remove soil.

Gradually fill the hole with the excavated soil, gently bouncing the plant up and down to ensure gaps between the roots are filled with soil. When the hole is refilled, firm the ground with your foot. Water and mulch the tree with a 5cm (2in) layer of well-rotted compost, garden compost or leafmould.

STAKING TREES

Trees up to 1m (3ft) in height don't need staking, while those taller than that will need supporting. Use stakes set vertically in the ground for bare-root trees and stakes at 45 degrees for container-grown ones. Secure with plastic buckle ties. Remove the stakes after 18 months, when the trees should be well anchored in the ground.

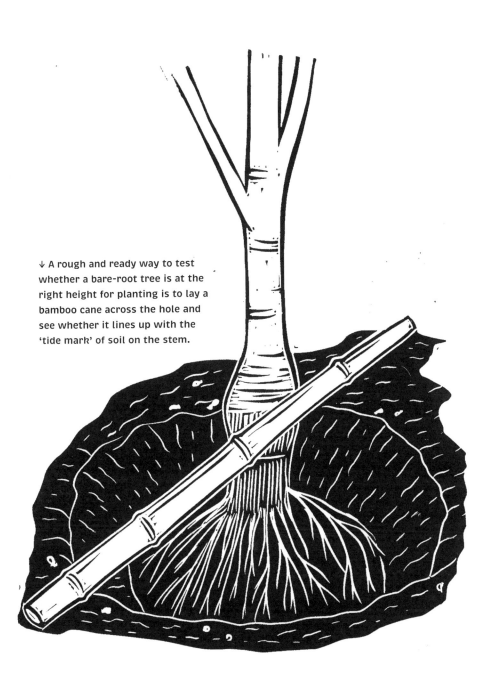

↓ A rough and ready way to test whether a bare-root tree is at the right height for planting is to lay a bamboo cane across the hole and see whether it lines up with the 'tide mark' of soil on the stem.

Make a Home for Wildlife

Turn your space into a miniature nature reserve by adding habitats for hibernation and daytime protection. In the wild, frogs, toads, beetles and hedgehogs love to shelter in piles of rotting logs. Create a log pile in your own garden by loosely arranging a few old branches together. Do this in a shady place such as under a tree, at the base of a hedge or behind the shed. Alternatively, make a habitat for insects, beetles and other small creatures with piles of stones.

Wall-mounted boxes come in a host of different shapes and sizes, and some have been designed to attract specific creatures. For example, there are bee houses, ladybird houses, lacewing chambers, mason bee nests and butterfly houses. A general bug box filled with pieces of bark, short lengths of bamboo cane, leaves and other materials will entice a wide range of mini-beasts such as ladybirds, spiders, lacewings and solitary bees. Boxes are best mounted facing north, so any hibernating inhabitants are not woken up too early by sunshine in spring, when the very few aphids, whitefly and other small insects they like to eat are not around. Make sure the box is angled slightly downward to prevent rain from entering.

Trivia time

According to flower lore, October's birth flower is the pot marigold. Symbolizing devotion and commitment, its botanical name of *Calendula* is derived from the Latin word *calends*, meaning the 'first day of every month' and is a nod to the plant flowering all year round in mild regions. The Latin word has given us the English word calendar.

PROJECT: How to Install Training Wires on a Fence

There are loads of ways to make supports for your fence, but here's a tried-and-tested method for creating a bank of parallel wires that run horizontally up the fence, spaced 30cm (12in) apart. Start with the first, 30cm (12in) from the ground.

YOU WILL NEED

- drill and drill bits ∘ eye bolts ∘ 12-gauge galvanized wire
- pliers ∘ adjustable spanner

HOW TO DO IT

1 Mark the positions for each horizontal wire at either end of the fence and drill through the two holes.

2 Push an eye bolt through each hole and secure loosely with its nut.

3 Thread the wire through the first eye, then bend it back, leaving a small amount of wire that can be twisted to hold it in place.

4 Unwind the wire across to the second eye bolt and cut it with pliers, leaving about 10cm (4cm) of excess. Thread through the second eye, then take up the slack by pulling the wire and securing it by twisting.

5 Use an adjustable spanner to tighten both bolts, to pull the wires tight. Don't overdo it or you'll put too much strain on the fence.

6 Repeat for the remaining parallel wires.

Make a Pond

A pond is an attractive feature that can be adapted to suit any garden. It can be any shape or size but looks best with an outline consisting of sweeping curves and not straight lines. The centre needs to be 60-100cm (2-3ft) deep, while one-third of the edge should have gently sloping sides, to allow access for wildlife. The remaining perimeter should include some wide 'shelves' for standing plants in pots.

Mark out the shape of the pond by trickling sand over the ground, and then excavate. Start by forming the marginal planting shelf, 15cm (6in) deep and 23cm (9in) wide, before digging out the rest of the pond. Pick out stones from the bottom, spread soft sand over the flat surfaces and then fit a flexible liner. Fill the pond with water and plant up in spring.

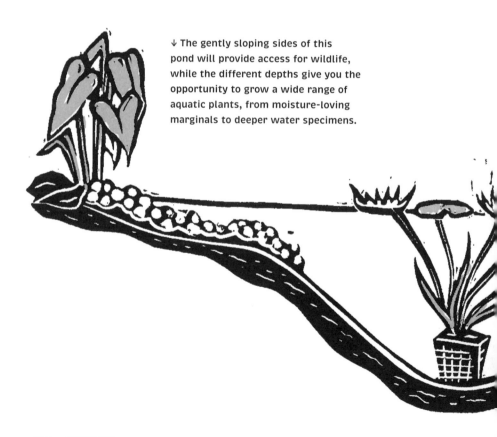

↓ The gently sloping sides of this pond will provide access for wildlife, while the different depths give you the opportunity to grow a wide range of aquatic plants, from moisture-loving marginals to deeper water specimens.

BUYING POND LINER

Liners come in prepacked sizes or can be cut to length from rolls. To work out how much material you will need, measure the length and width of the pond hole. Then measure the depth and multiply by two. Add this figure to the length and to the width, and then multiply the final length and width measurements.

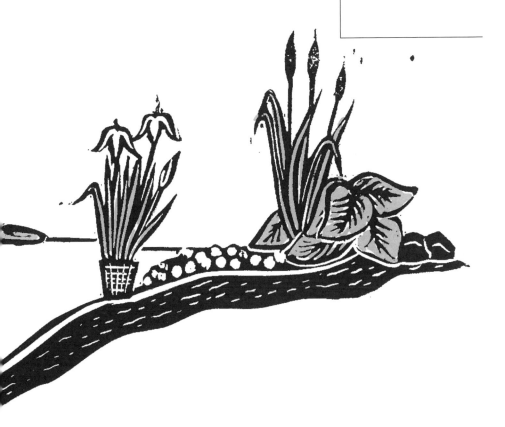

Deal with Self-seeders

To keep beds and borders under control, spend a few minutes hoicking out self-seeded plants. Many perennials, shrubs and trees sow seed prolifically, and the seedlings that follow will be popping up everywhere. Although a few self-seeded plants can give a garden a natural look, most will invariably grow where you don't want them or will crowd out other plants. The answer is to carry out some ruthless editing. If you feel guilty about despatching these young plants, prise them up carefully with a garden fork (ensuring you remove a good rootball of soil), then pot them up and give them away.

Grow Climbers

There are masses of climbers that will cling, twine or use tendrils to scale walls, fences and other vertical structures, elevating gardens with their attractive flowers, foliage or fruit. Climbing roses (*Rosa*), honeysuckles (*Lonicera*), trumpet vine (*Campis*), clematis and potato vine (*Solanum laxum*) will thrive in sun, while schizophragma, *Pileostegia viburnoides* and ivy (*Hedera*) will do well in more dimly lit places. Some climbers are self-clinging, yet the majority will need some form of support as they grow. Possible supports include wooden trellis panels, training wires and decorative screens.

PLANTING CLIMBERS

The soil close to walls, fences and other structures tends to be on the dry side, so plant climbers about 30cm (12in) away from your chosen supports to ensure the roots will be in moist ground. Dig a hole that's the same depth as the rootball and twice as wide. Take the plant out of its pot and tease out some of the roots if they are congested. Place the climber in the centre of the hole, making sure the top of the rootball is level with the surface. Backfill the hole with soil, firming as you go. Arrange three canes in a fan shape, at a 45-degree angle, toward the vertical surface. Carefully untie the climber from its original cane support and secure individual shoots to the fan of canes, using soft twine. Water well, to ensure the roots and surrounding soil are moist.

PLANT CLEMATIS DEEPLY

Clematis need planting with the top of the rootball 5cm (2in) beneath the surface of the soil. Planting deeply acts as an insurance against clematis wilt, a fungal disease that can cause stems to flag and die. If the stems succumb, then they can be cut to the ground, allowing healthy shoots to appear from beneath the soil. Spread a 5cm (2in) layer of garden compost or leafmould over the soil, to help keep the roots cool, leaving a 7.5cm (3in) gap around the stems.

↓ The soil closest to walls and fences is often dry due to being in a rain shadow. Planting climbers 30cm (12in) away from vertical surfaces means their roots have a better chance of being sated by rainwater.

Sow Broad Beans

Broad beans are often started in early spring but there are several advantages to getting them going in autumn. They'll germinate quickly and develop into young plants before the arrival of winter. Plants will then romp away when temperatures increase in spring, providing pickings much earlier than those sown in March or April. Perhaps the biggest benefit of sowing now is that plants should avoid the attention of blackfly, which can infest stems, leaves, flowers and pods. These sap-suckers are drawn towards the young shoots and will leave the woodier stems of older plants alone.

HOW TO SOW

Broad beans prefer light, stone-free soil in a sunny spot. Prepare the ground by digging, removing weeds and large stones, and then rake to leave a fine finish. Make a 5cm (2in)-deep trench and sow seeds 23cm (9in) apart, leaving a gap of 60cm (2ft) between rows. Cover with soil and water well. Sow a few extra seeds at the end of each row to act as a safeguard against any not germinating within the rows. These can be lifted and replanted in gaps, if necessary.

NATIONAL GARDEN FESTIVALS

Five national garden festivals were held in Britain during the 1980s and early '90s. Running from 2 May until 14 October 1984, the first event in Liverpool featured a giant yellow submarine in honour of The Beatles. It can now be found on display at the city's airport.

- 1984 – Liverpool
- 1986 – Stoke-on-Trent
- 1988 – Glasgow
- 1990 – Gateshead
- 1992 – Ebbw Vale

'Judge each day not by the harvest you reap but by the seeds you plant.'

William Arthur Ward

WHAT TO DO NEXT

Keep plants well-watered, especially when the pods appear and during dry periods. Pinch out the growing tips of plants as the pods begin to develop, to encourage them to produce more beans. If you sow a variety that grows over 45cm (18in) tall, shore up the stems with garden canes and lengths of string.

HOW TO HARVEST

The pods are ready for picking once you can see the beans starting to swell inside – remove a pod and split it open to check the seeds' progress before committing to harvesting a handful. To remove the pod, pull back against the direction it is growing and twist off, taking care not to tear the stem. Another option is to snip it off with scissors or secateurs.

THREE GREAT BROAD BEAN VARIETIES HARDY ENOUGH FOR SOWING IN AUTUMN

1 'Aquadulce Claudia' - a heritage variety that produces masses of 23cm (9in)-long pods.

2 'Superaguadulce' - one of the hardiest of all varieties, this produces 75cm (30in)-high plants that carry 20cm (8in)-long pods filled with up to nine white beans.

3 'The Sutton' - a fantastic dwarf variety that was introduced by Devon-based Suttons Seeds in 1923. Plants grow to only around 30cm (12in) and have 12cm (5in)-long pods that contain five or six beans with a delicious flavour.

A POTTED HISTORY OF BROAD BEANS

Native to the Mediterranean, broad beans have been cultivated for at least 10,000 years. They found their way to Britain during the Iron Age and were the most popular bean on our shores until runner beans arrived from the New World during the 17th century. It's believed broad beans were eaten by Celtic people at funeral feasts, giving us the terms beanfeast and beano.

Get Going with Garlic

There are lots of different varieties of garlic, and these have flavours that range from mild to something so powerful that it would repel a vampire. Raising your own garlic crop from scratch is very easy, and cloves planted in autumn will form large bulbs that will be ready for lifting early next summer. Always start with virus-free bulbs bought from garden centres or online specialists. Don't use culinary garlic bulbs from shops, as they are sometimes treated with chemicals to prevent them from sprouting.

CHOOSING WHAT TO GROW

Garlic is divided into two groups: soft necks and hard necks. Soft necks form a mass of flexible strappy leaves in the ground, which rise above each bulb with a white papery skin that encloses lots of small cloves. They can be stored for months after harvesting. Hard necks develop a stiff stalk that is topped with a flowerhead. Bulbs often don't have an outer skin and the cloves are fewer but larger in size. Unfortunately, hard-neck garlic doesn't store as well as soft neck and so is best used soon after lifting.

TOP TIP

If you're strapped for space, plant garlic in 30–45cm (12–18in) pots filled with peat-free potting compost, adding some horticultural grit for drainage. Space cloves about 10cm (4in) apart.

DID YOU KNOW ?

During a special episode of *MasterChef Australia* in 2018, the Duchess of Cornwall admitted that eating garlic is a 'no-no' with the royal family. Former royal chef Darren McGrady once revealed to *Marie Claire* magazine that 'the Queen would never have garlic on the menu. She hated the smell of it; she hated the taste of it.'

FIVE GREAT GARLIC VARIETIES TO TRY

1 **'Chesnok Red'** - a hard-neck variety with purple-striped bulbs containing strong-flavoured cloves.

2 **'Edenrose'** - is admired for its delicate taste and was bred in France; this hard-neck variety has rose-skinned cloves that show up well through the outer white casing.

3 **'Provence Wight'** - boasts large white bulbs that are packed with sweet fat cloves, which can be stored until January; it is a soft-neck variety.

4 **'Purple Wight'** - a soft-neck variety with strong-flavoured cloves that are wrapped in purple and white bulbs.

5 **'Red Sicilian'** - has pink- and white-skinned bulbs full of spicy cloves; it is a hard-neck variety.

HOW TO GROW GARLIC

Prepare the soil for planting by digging over and raking until the texture resembles coarse breadcrumbs - a spot that gets plenty of sunshine is perfect. Carefully remove the papery outer casing from the bulbs and then split them into individual cloves, leaving the tight skin intact. Keep only fat healthy cloves and reject any that are soft, mouldy or have any visible signs of damage. Make small holes, 20cm (8in) apart, pop a clove in each and bury with soil, making sure the pointy end is just beneath the surface. Water well. Garlic will be ready for harvesting in summer, when the leaves start to turn yellow.

Blackberries in Pots

Many blackberries are vigorous vicious things that are unsuitable for small gardens. However, recent breeding work has led to a number of compact thornless varieties that are good for growing in large containers. Plant upright varieties in 45cm (18in)-wide containers filled with a 50:50 mix of peat-free, multipurpose potting compost and John Innes No 3. Train shoots against a fan of trellis or add a circular cage support. Water plants regularly during the growing season, especially during dry spells, and feed in mid-spring with a high-potash fertilizer to ensure a heavy crop of fruit. Cut fruited shoots to the ground in autumn.

FOUR GREAT BLACKBERRY VARIETIES TO GROW IN POTS

1 **'Black Cascade'** - is a real novelty with its 45cm (18in)-long, trailing branches and is perfect for a hanging basket.

2 **'Loch Maree'** - boasts masses of pink flowers followed by heavy crops of fruit, which will provide pickings from summer until mid-autumn.

3 **'Merton Thornless'** - developed by the John Innes Horticultural Institute and launched in 1941, this has prickle-free stems and fruit measuring up to 2.5cm (1in) across.

4 **'Waldo'** - a compact performer that grows to 1.5m (5ft) in height, its thornless stems bear lots of glossy berries in August and September.

HEALTH BENEFITS OF BLACKBERRIES
Blackberries have impressive health benefits. The fruit are a good source of vitamins A, B, C and E, and are high in nutrients like potassium, magnesium and calcium. High in fibre that helps to reduce cholesterol, they are also low in calories, carbohydrates and fat.

Plant Blueberries

They may have an exotic air but anyone can raise their own crop of blueberries by planting a shrub in the ground or a container. There are loads of different varieties which range in height from 30cm (12in) to 2.1m (7ft), bearing fruit between early July and late September, depending on the variety. Most are deciduous, although a few are evergreen.

BONUS FEATURES

Apart from supplying you with handfuls of delicious fruit, blueberry plants work hard to earn their keep. Shrubs boast masses of scented, bell-shaped, ivory-coloured flowers in spring, and deciduous types have foliage that turns bright red before falling in autumn. In winter, these plants make a good substitute for dogwoods (*Cornus*), thanks to their vibrant red stems.

GROWING BLUEBERRIES

Blueberries like a sunny spot and acidic soil. If you don't have the right type of soil, compact varieties are perfect in pots filled with lime-free compost - a mix containing plenty of composted bark is best. Water using rainwater stored in a butt (only use tap water as a last resort during periods of drought) and feed in spring with lime-free fertilizer granules.

SUCCESSFUL POLLINATION

Many blueberry varieties are self-pollinating and a single plant will usually produce a decent crop of fruit. However, for even better yields it's generally recommended that two or even three different varieties that flower at the same time are planted close together to allow cross-pollination. If you only have room for one plant, choose a variety that's renowned for being self-fertile, such as 'Bluecrop', 'Chandler' and 'Sunshine Blue'.

HEALTH BENEFITS OF BLUEBERRIES

One of the first foods to be given superfood status, blueberries have high levels of antioxidants and are a good source of vitamin C, manganese and dietary fibre.

HARVESTING AND STORAGE

Blueberries are ready for picking when plump and slightly soft to the touch. Remove by gently pulling them away from branches and eat immediately or store in the refrigerator for about ten days. Place in a single layer and not in a pile, as the weight will cause bruising, leading to rotting. Frozen berries will last for up to six months.

PRUNING TIPS

Keep blueberries healthy, productive and within bounds by trimming them between late winter and early spring. Remove dead, diseased or damaged growth, along with any older branches that are no longer productive - shoots of four years old or more tend to run out of steam. At the same time, snip back overly long shoots, to maintain an attractive shape

UNDERPLANTING BLUEBERRIES

Rather than waste the space at the bottom of containers, it's a good idea to make the most of the lime-free compost by growing other plants that thrive in similar conditions. One of the best edible choices are cranberries (*Vaccinium macrocarpon*), which are low-growing, trailing vines that will spread over the surface and cascade down the sides of the pot. Plants have attractive pink flowers, dark red berries in autumn and their foliage is evergreen, providing interest all year round. Other options include lingonberries (*Vaccinium vitis-idaea*) and strawberries (*Fragaria*), including alpine ones.

A POTTED HISTORY OF BLUEBERRIES

Blueberries (*Vaccinium corymbosum*) are originally from North America, especially the area covered by the state of New Jersey. The fruit was held in high esteem by native Americans, who called them star berries, because of the five-pointed shape on the bottom of each fruit. Apart from gathering berries to eat, they used blueberry juice both as a cough medicine and as a dye for clothes. A tea brewed from the leaves was thought to purify the blood and was taken by pregnant women to help trigger childbirth.

FIVE GREAT BLUEBERRY VARIETIES TO TRY

1 'Chandler' - a large shrub that produces fruit the size of a cherry for about six weeks from early summer. H × S: 2 × 2m (6½ × 6½ft).

2 'Herbert' - dating back to 1953, it produces good crops of large, aromatic and tasty fruit that ripens in late July. H × S: 1.2 × 1.5m (4 × 5ft).

3 'Patriot' - forms a fairly compact bush with dark blue berries early in the season; it's extremely cold hardy. H × S: 1.2 × 1.2m (4 × 4ft).

4 'Flamingo' - introduced in 2019, this boasts dazzling, pink-splashed foliage and bears berries from June until the end of July. H × S: 100 × 70cm (39 × 28in).

5 'Pink Lemonade' - sometimes sold as 'Pink Sapphire', this has pink flowers in spring and sweet, bright pink fruit in late summer. H × S: 1.5 × 1.5m (5 × 5ft).

Pest and Disease Watch: Apple Scab

This common fungal disease leads to leaves becoming splattered with dark spots and scabby patches developing on the skin of fruit. Although destroying infected fruit and fallen leaves will reduce the amount of fungal spores that overwinter, it won't prevent the disease from coming back. If problems persist, replace with a scab-resistant variety such as 'Egremont Russet', 'Kidd's Orange Red' or 'Ashmead's Kernel'.

FLOWERS IN SONGS

Garden flowers have long provided inspiration for many song writers. Here are a few album tracks and singles from a range of different artists:

- **Gladiolus Rag** - Scott Joplin (1907)

- **Scarlet Begonias** - Grateful Dead (1974)

- **Forget Me Nots** - Patrice Rushen (1982)

- **Iris** - The Breeders (1990)

- **Marigold** - Nirvana (1992)

- **Sunflower** - Paul Weller (1993)

- **Daffodil Lament** - The Cranberries (1994)

- **Anemone** - Brian Jonestown Massacre (1996)

- **Gardenia** - Iggy Pop (2016)

- **Daisy** - Pond (2019)

'In the other gardens

And all up the vale,

From the autumn bonfires

See the smoke trail!'

(Robert Louis Stevenson, *Autumn Fires*)

THE MONTH AT A GLANCE

- Plant bare-root trees, shrubs and roses (see Bare-root Plants, page 216).
- Wrap up exotic plants for winter (see Protect Exotics, page 218).
- Remove any large figs left on plants as they are unlikely to ripen (see When Do Figs Produce Fruit, page 36).
- Pick autumn leaves from the crowns of alpines and late-flowering bulbs, to prevent plants from rotting.
- Plant bare-root wallflowers (*Erysimum cheiri*) (see Ways with Wallflowers, page 224).
- Take hardwood cuttings (see page 226).
- Plant tulip bulbs (see page 222).
- Pot up cuttings of pelargoniums, fuchsias and other tender perennials taken in the summer.
- Plant raspberry canes (see Grow Raspberries, page 227).
- Tidy up veg patches (see page 220).
- Check stored potatoes for blight disease.
- Cover brassicas with netting, to protect from pigeons.
- Insulate containers, to protect against cold snaps (see Prepare Containers for Winter, page 212).
- Collect deciduous leaves, to make leafmould (see Make a Leafmould Bin, page 214).
- Stand patio containers on pot feet, to improve drainage.
- Cover compost bins with sheets of cardboard, to maintain temperatures inside.
- Paint fences, sheds and wooden structures with preservative, during spells of dry bright weather.
- Remove branches infected with coral spots from trees and shrubs (see Pest and Disease Watch: Coral Spot, page 225).
- Insulate greenhouses with sheets of UV-stabilized bubble wrap (see Fit Insulation, page 215).
- Wipe the leaves of dusty houseplants with a damp cloth, to help plants make the most of lower light levels.

November

November always arrives with a bang. Quite literally, actually. Early in the month, the garden air reverberates to the booms, whistles and crackling of fireworks as many folk celebrate Guy Fawkes Night. As the leaves start to fall in earnest from the branches of trees and shrubs, the garden begins to look a little wintry - it's a sign that this is time to prepare the plot for colder weather to come.

Prepare Containers for Winter

Plants in pots don't have it easy. Plummeting temperatures, frost and rain can really take their toll on foliage and roots, while a hard frost can lead to expensive terra-cotta or ceramic pots cracking and falling apart. Gardeners with a greenhouse can move vulnerable plants inside until spring, but there are ways to protect those that have to remain outdoors.

INSULATE POTS

Frost can easily penetrate the sides of containers and kill roots or cause the pot surfaces to crack, so wrap the entire exterior with a piece of hessian, bubble wrap or horticultural fleece, ensuring that it's held securely in place with garden twine - keep the top of the pot free from the protective material for watering.

TENDER SPECIMENS

An easy way to protect plants that aren't fully hardy, or those with flower buds vulnerable to frost early in the year is to slip a fleece 'jacket' over the top - a drawstring at the base prevents it blowing off in the wind. Alternatively, simply wrap the top of the plant with a sheet of fleece held in place with twine.

IMPROVE DRAINAGE

Plants in pots are vulnerable to excessive moisture. Prevent problems by raising them off the ground on 'pot feet' or by using stones or bricks. This will allow excess moisture to escape through the drainage holes, while the gap underneath will give plants a boost, providing better air circulation to the root area.

GIVE PLANTS SHELTER

Place plants next to a sheltered wall of your house until spring. Apart from helping to protect them from too much rain, this spot will be slightly warmer than other parts of the garden. Pack plants in tightly together so they help to insulate each other, and run a strip of bubble wrap around the outside of the containers.

Trivia time

The concept of the garden centre arrived in Britain in 1953. Inspired by a business trip to the USA, where plants and gardening accessories were sold in self-service stores, the managing director of Waterers Nursery in Surrey organized for a stand to be built at the Chelsea Flower Show that featured plants in pots with detailed growing instructions.

↓ Make sure pot feet are spaced out evenly to prevent containers toppling over during windy weather.

PROJECT: Make a Leafmould Bin

Fallen leaves can be turned into leafmould, a dark crumbly material that makes a good soil improver or mulch. If you have a large garden, make a square cage with 1m (3ft) sides for leaves. Use four stakes surrounded by chicken wire and site the bin on grass or soil for drainage. Add leaves regularly and cover with a waterproof sheet.

YOU WILL NEED

- Mallet ○ 4 x 1.2m (4ft) stakes ○ Chicken wire
- U-shaped galvanised staples ○ Hammer ○ Wire cutters ○ Leaves
- Waterproof sheet

HOW TO DO IT

1 Use a mallet to knock each tree stake 20cm (8in) into the ground, forming a square shape with each post set 1m (3ft) apart.

2 Attach the edge of the chicken wire to a post, hammering it into place with U-shaped staples.

3 Unroll the chicken wire around the next post and secure with staples. Continue in this way until you reach the last post.

4 Pull the chicken wire tightly around the last post and cut to size with wire cutters. Finish by attaching it to the post with U-shaped staples. Fill with leaves and cover with the waterproof sheet.

USING LEAFMOULD

By the time next autumn arrives, the leaves will have changed into a crumbly material that is ideal as a mulch. Leave the leafmould another year and it will rot down even further, to make a dark brown compost, which can be dug into the ground as a soil conditioner. This material contains high levels of humus, which helps soil to retain moisture and enables it to hold onto nutrients.

Get Greenhouses Winter-ready

This combination of potting shed, shelter for tender plants, storage depot and place to tinker about when the weather is poor really comes into its own during the winter months. To ensure it fulfils its potential, give the greenhouse some attention to get it winter-ready.

IMPROVE LIGHT LEVELS

Clean the glass to allow as much light as possible to penetrate. Scrub both the exterior and interior with soapy water, using a telescopic cleaning device to reach the ridge. At the same time, scoop out debris that has accumulated in gutters, to ensure they are free running.

CLEAN THE INSIDE

On a dry day, move all of the contents of the greenhouse outside, covering plants with fleece if it's chilly. Sweep the floor, benches and shelves to remove leaves and compost. Apart from making the greenhouse look untidy, debris can harbour diseases and makes a snug place for pests to hunker down.

FIT INSULATION

Fix sheets of UV-stabilized bubble wrap to the inside of the greenhouse. Use scissors to cut the insulation material to size, fitting pieces to the sides, roof, ends and door. Hold in place with all-weather tape or plastic clips that fit into the grooves of glazing bars. Attach bubble wrap to wooden greenhouses with drawing pins.

ADD A HEATER

A heater is essential to keep greenhouses frost-free. If you have an outdoor socket, plug in an electric fan heater, running it at 10°C (50°F). A small paraffin or gas heater makes a basic alternative; turn it off during the day if the weather is mild, and make sure you stock up on fuel so you don't run out during a cold snap.

LIGHT IT UP

Some kind of light is a must in a greenhouse, to allow pottering on overcast days or after dark. Among the most suitable types are LED battery-powered pull lights and electric lamps fitted with fluorescent tubes. Ideally, position in the centre of the structure, making sure the lightning is above head height.

Bare-root Plants

Before the invention of plastic pots, trees and shrubs were available only from late autumn until early spring. Grown in fields, they were lifted while dormant and sold as 'bare roots'. These days, container-grown trees and shrubs are ubiquitous, but bare roots are still widely available. A big advantage of these is that they are cheaper than their container-grown counterparts.

PREPARING FOR PLANTING

Prior to planting, put bare-root plants in a bucket of water for a few hours, to ensure the roots are fully hydrated. After they are well soaked, check for any damage - trim away any branches or roots that are torn, damaged or diseased. If bad weather interrupts planting, dig a hole and plunge the plants into it, making sure the roots are covered with soil.

PLANTING BARE-ROOT PLANTS

Bare-root plants can be planted at any time during their dormant season, as long as the ground isn't frozen or waterlogged. Plant them at the same depth as they were growing before being lifted from the ground - there should be an obvious 'tide mark' of soil on the trunk. Dig a square hole that's twice the diameter of the root system and deep enough so the mark on the trunk lines up with the ground surface. Position the plant in the hole, checking again that it is at the appropriate depth. Then replace the soil and gently firm the plant into place with your heel. Finish by giving it a good soaking.

THE LANGUAGE OF BARE-ROOT PLANTS

Seedlings are one-year-old trees, while transplants are grown in a seedbed and then moved to the open ground. They are usually bushy and sold when they are 0.6-1.2m (2-4ft) tall. Whips are also transplants but with a single stem, 1-2m (3-6½ft) tall. Standing 1.8-2.5m (6-8ft) in height, feathered trees have side branches that go down to ground level. Half-standard trees have 1.2-1.5m (4-5ft) of clear stem before the branches start, while standard trees have 1.8-2m (6-6½ft) of clear stem.

'If a tree dies, plant another in its place.'

Carl Linnaeus

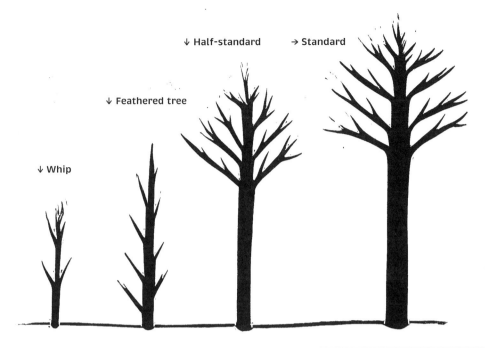

↓ Whip   ↓ Feathered tree   ↓ Half-standard   → Standard

WHAT NEXT?

Bare-root plants can lose up to 90 percent of their original root system when they are lifted from the ground. As a result, don't expect too much in their first year - shoots are likely to be shorter and leaves smaller than normal. In their second year, the roots will have spread, enabling plants to take up more water and nutrients, thus promoting better top growth. Expect vigorous growth from the third year onward.

Look After Alpines

True alpine plants happily put up with sub-zero temperatures but they can soon turn up their toes in wet winters. Excessive moisture around the crown of plants can cause fungal diseases, while damp soil can result in roots rotting. If you have only a few plants, cover them with plastic cloches. Groups of alpines can be protected by making a shelter from two columns of bricks with a sheet of clear rigid plastic placed over the top. Over the next few months, remove any leaves that blow onto plants, to ensure light reaches them, and deadhead spent flowers, if necessary.

Name explain:
Mahonia

Mahonias are shrubs native to the Himalayas and east Asia, along with North and Central America. They were given their botanical name by English botanist Thomas Nuttall, who worked in America. It honours his friend Bernhard McMahon, an Irish nurseryman who emigrated to Philadelphia in 1796 and was gardening mentor to the third US president Thomas Jefferson.

Protect Exotics

Architectural specimens and exotics are vulnerable to winter weather. Frost, snow, rain and gusty blasts can really knock the stuffing out of these plants, resulting in their demise or causing long-lasting damage to foliage, shoots and roots. To ensure they make it through to spring unscathed, take measures to protect vulnerable plants from the worst of the weather.

BAMBOOS

Many bamboos can take a cold snap of -20°C (-4°F) or more, but plants can be damaged by strong winds. In order to keep them upright, encircle the entire clump with rope and secure to a stake hammered into the ground. A heavy downfall of snow can cause the canes to bow and even break, so shake off carefully before the snow has a chance to freeze solid, using a garden cane or broom if necessary.

BANANAS

The stems of Japanese bananas (*Musa basjoo*) will die back if temperatures fall to 0°C (32°F), so protect plants with an insulated cage. Remove all leaves and then cut straight across the top of the trunk with a pruning saw, to leave a clear stem. Hammer a tree stake into the ground, 15cm (6in) away from the trunk. Fold a piece of chicken wire around the trunk and secure with cable ties, to make a circular cage. Fill the void with some straw and place an old compost bag on top to keep out the rain, securing it with garden twine.

TREE FERNS

If your garden is protected or you live in a mild area where frost is unlikely, all you need do is wedge a handful of straw in the top of the plant to protect the nascent fronds. In exposed gardens, give ferns greater protection, to prevent foliage from browning off and dying. Pull the fronds up vertically, tie them together with garden twine, then wrap with horticultural fleece. Hold securely with more twine.

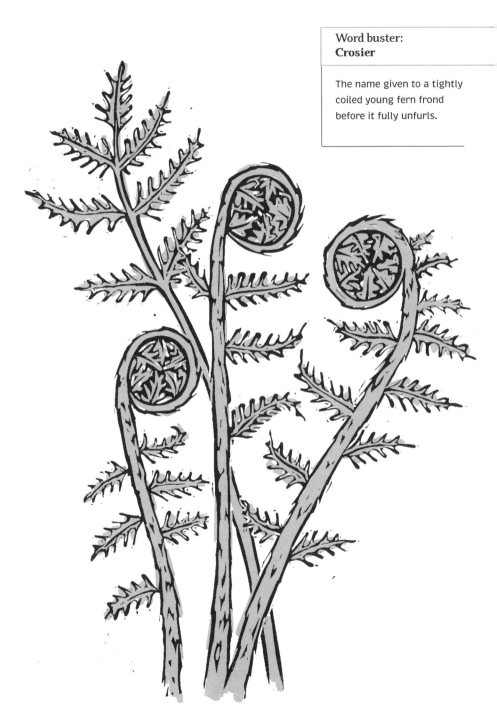

TENDER BULBS

Dahlias, Indian shot plant (*Canna*) and other summer-flowering beauties that grow from rhizomes, tubers or bulbs will quickly turn to mush if you have an exposed garden or heavy soil that is soggy over winter. In these situations, cut back the top growth and carefully lift the plant from the ground. Put in a tray of dry compost and store in a frost-free place until next spring. If you have a sheltered plot or lighter soil, you can leave such tender plants in the soil, but cover them with a 7.5cm (3in) layer of garden compost, to keep frost away from the roots.

CORDYLINES

Cabbage palm (*Cordyline australis*) suffers when frost damages the bark, leading to stems rotting and eventually collapsing. To ensure their survival, pull the leaves up vertically and bind together firmly. Finish by encircling the entire plant with several layers of well secured horticultural fleece.

PALMS

Many palms are as tough as old boots and in mild areas they rarely need protecting, especially when mature. In colder areas, stuff a handful of straw into the crown, then wrap the trunk with hessian or horticultural fleece and secure it. Spread a 7.5cm (3in) layer of garden compost, composted bark or similar material around the base to protect the roots from frost.

Tidy Up Veg Patches

Put veg patches to bed before winter arrives. Start by pulling up the remains of tomatoes, sweetcorn and other annual crops to prevent them rotting and acting as an entry point for pests and diseases. Chop up stems into small bits and add to the compost heap. Cut off the stems of beans and peas to ground level and leave the nitrogen-fixing roots in situ to feed next year's crops. Dismantle wigwams, A-frame bean supports and similar structures; wipe the soil from them and then stash in a shed or another dry place. If you grew crops in pots, decant the compost and scrub the containers with warm soapy water. Store once dry.

Add Some Two-tone Plants

Variegated plants are a bit like Marmite. Some gardeners love them so much that they will happily elbow all sorts of plants with patterned leaves into every available gap, while others consider them the height of bad taste and refuse to allow them through the front gate. Despite polarizing gardeners, there's no doubt that variegated plants add some spice to the planting mix. When picked with care and used sparingly, such plants help to illuminate poorly lit spots, lead the eye through a scheme and add definition to borders. Variegated evergreens are particularly invaluable in winter, providing a shot of colour when very little else is around. It's important not to cram too many variegated plants into your garden, as the effect will be chaotic. Use the odd variegated evergreen shrub to add punch to a bed or a splash of light to a dull corner.

FIVE VARIEGATED PLANTS FOR WINTER COLOUR

1   *Daphne odora* 'Aureomarginata' - a compact shrub with yellow-edged leaves and scented pink blooms from early spring.

2   *Elaeagnus × submacrophylla* 'Gilt Edge' - a tough shrub for sun or semi-shade, with two-tone, gold and dark green leaves.

3   *Hedera algeriensis* 'Gloire de Marengo' - this Algerian ivy has large, silvery green leaves with creamy yellow margins.

4   *Ilex × altaclerensis* 'Golden King' - this holly boasts near spineless, oval green leaves with wide golden margins.

5   *Viburnum tinus* 'Variegatum' - a shrub with yellow and green leaves, and white flowers throughout winter and early spring.

DIFFERENT TYPES OF VARIEGATION

The patterns of variegation are diverse. Some plants have leaves that are lightly speckled or heavily spotted, while others boast a bold splash of colour in the centre or have leaves with different-coloured margins – this can vary from thin to very wide, almost covering half the leaf. Elsewhere, leaves might be striped, marbled or have different-coloured veins. Some display random patches of colour, giving each leaf an irregular look.

WHAT CAUSES VARIEGATION

Variegation is usually caused by a mutation that prevents or inhibits cells from producing chlorophyll, the green pigment essential for photosynthesis. Complete lack of chlorophyll leads to white areas forming, while orange, yellow and light green variegation results from reduced production of chlorophyll. There are very few examples of variegated plants in nature, and most are borne in cultivation, usually from variegated shoots that appear on pure green plants.

Plant Tulip Bulbs

Most spring bulbs can be planted any time from late summer until early winter but November is the best time to plant tulips (*Tulipa*). Tulip bulbs don't form roots until the weather turns colder, and there's less chance of them being hit by tulip fire - a fungal disease that disfigures both flowers and foliage.

Although the general rule when planting bulbs is to dig holes two or three times their own depth, with tulips the holes should be 15-20cm (6-8in) deep, to protect the bulbs from fungal diseases. Choose a sunny spot with well-drained soil. Space bulbs 5-10cm (2-4in) apart and add some sharp grit to the base of planting holes, to improve drainage.

DID YOU KNOW ?

Native to parts of the Middle East and Central Asia, tulip bulbs arrived during the 1500s in Holland, where botanists bred some novel varieties that were highly desirable. A Dutch craze for tulips in the 1630s saw bulbs exchanging hands for absurd sums of money in a period that's become known as Tulipomania. The enthusiasm for tulips was embraced by the whole of Europe, with bulbs even being traded on the London Stock Exchange. Trading was buoyant until the market collapsed in February 1637, when tulip bulbs became virtually worthless overnight.

Botanists have divided tulips into 15 groups based on the characteristics of their flowers. Here are the groups along with some examples:

group 1 - Single early tulips ('Apricot Beauty', 'Lac van Rijn', 'White Prince')

group 2 - Double early tulips ('Foxtrot', 'Mondial', 'Verona')

group 3 - Triumph tulips ('Algarve', 'Brown Sugar', 'Hermitage')

group 4 - Darwin hybrid tulips ('Apeldoorn', 'Daydream', 'Olympic Flame')

group 5 - Single late tulips ('Menton', 'Queen of Night', 'Sorbet')

group 6 - Lily-flowered tulips ('Ballerina', 'West Point', 'White Triumphator')

group 7 - Fringed tulips ('Blue Heaven', 'Davenport', 'Honeymoon')

group 8 - Viridiflora tulips ('Artist', 'China Town', 'Spring Green')

group 9 - Rembrandt tulips ('Black and White', 'Insulinde', 'The Lizard')

group 10 - Parrot tulips ('Estella Rijnveld', 'Green Wave', 'Rococo')

group 11 - Double late (peony-flowered) tulips ('Angélique', 'Orange Princess', 'Sun Lover')

group 12 - Kaufmanniana tulips ('Fashion', 'Johann Strauss', 'Stresa')

group 13 - Fosteriana tulips ('Orange Emperor', 'Purissima', 'Sweetheart')

group 14 - Greigii tulips ('Für Elise', 'Pinocchio', 'Toronto')

group 15 - Miscellaneous tulips ('Little Princess', 'Peppermintstick', T. sprengeri).

Ways with Wallflowers

Biennial wallflowers (*Erysimum cheiri*) are spring-flowering treasures that are widely available as bare-root plants in autumn. Available in shades of white, yellow, orange, red, pink and purple, the flowers of most are borne from buds in April and form dense heads that will provide a show for around six weeks. Apart from looking good, many possess a sweet scent.

After buying bare-root plants, soak them in a bucket of water, to ensure the roots are fully hydrated. Choose a sunny spot and dig holes that are deep enough to accommodate roots and spaced 15-20cm (6-8in) apart. Then pop in each plant, backfill with soil and firm in place with your fingers, ensuring the lower leaves are just above the surface.

THREE GREAT WALLFLOWER VARIETIES TO TRY

- **'Fire King'** – these bushy plants, 45cm (18in) high, will set the garden alight with their scented, orange-red blooms from March until the end of May.

- **Sugar Rush Series** – a mixture of vibrant shades that is sweetly scented, providing interest in autumn and again in spring, on bushy, 30cm (12in)-tall plants.

- **'Vulcan'** – named after the Roman god of fire, this hot variety produces 30cm (12in)-tall stems clothed with purplish buds that open into striking crimson flowers.

PLANT COMBINATIONS

Wallflowers combine brilliantly with other spring-interest plants. A classic partnership is to interplant them with late-flowering tulips (*Tulipa*). Wallflower 'Blood Red' makes a striking contrast with the green-striped tulip 'Formosa', while the wallflower 'Orange Bedder' and tulip 'Ballerina', with its orange blooms, will provide a splash of tonal harmony. Other options are to plant wallflowers with daffodils (*Narcissus*), forget-me-nots (*Myosotis*) and spurge (*Euphorbia*).

A POTTED HISTORY OF WALLFLOWERS

Wallflowers originate from North Africa, Asia and parts of Europe, where they can be found growing on cliffs and other rocky places. Nobody knows when they arrived in Britain, but they were a key feature of Elizabethan gardens and a popular ingredient of nosegays – small bunches of scented flowers carried by fashionable ladies to disguise bad smells in cities. The common name wallflower comes from the plant's ability to self-seed in inhospitable places.

Pest and Disease Watch: Coral Spot

This fungal disease attacks the dead or dying branches of deciduous trees and shrubs, and can easily be recognized by its raised orange spots. Prevent coral spot spreading to healthy wood by moving infected growth with secateurs and either burning or binning the debris.

Trivia time

The Royal Horticultural Society was founded as the Horticultural Society of London in 1804. Its first meeting was held at Hatchard's bookshop on Piccadilly and was attended by seven prominent horticulturists and keen gardeners, including Sir Joseph Banks and William Forsyth.

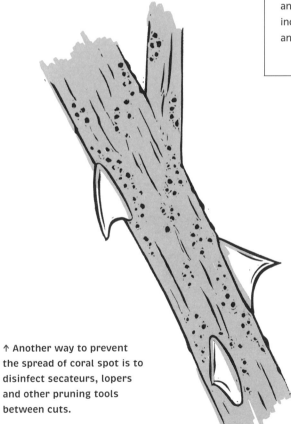

↑ Another way to prevent the spread of coral spot is to disinfect secateurs, lopers and other pruning tools between cuts.

Take Hardwood Cuttings

Taking hardwood cuttings is a simple way of propagating a wide range of deciduous trees, shrubs and climbers at a time when plants are dormant, from late autumn to the end of winter. Select a few strong, straight shoots of pencil thickness and divide these into pieces, 15-23cm (6-9in) long. Use secateurs to make a straight cut above a pair of buds, followed by an angled cut just above another set of buds. The slanted cut will help you identify which end needs to be planted upright and also allows it to shed water.

Make a 15cm (6in)-deep trench with one straight side and spread some grit along the base. Insert cuttings every 10cm (4in) along its length, with two-thirds below ground. Top up the trench with soil, then firm and water.

Alternatively, place several cuttings in pots filled with equal parts peat-free, multipurpose potting compost and coarse grit.

WHAT TO TAKE HARDWOOD CUTTINGS OF

- blackcurrant
- dogwood (*Cornus*)
- elder (*Sambucus*)
- fig (*Ficus*)
- forsythia
- gooseberry
- honeysuckle (*Lonicera*)
- jasmine (*Jasminum*)
- mock orange (*Philadelphus*)
- willow (*Salix*)

ART IN THE GARDEN

Gardens have provided inspiration for some of our best-loved artists. Here are a few you can visit:

- **William Morris**, Red House, Bexleyheath, Kent

- **Henry Moore**, Hoglands, Perry Green, Hertfordshire

- **Derek Jarman**, Prospect Cottage, Dungeness, Kent

- **Barbara Hepworth**, Trewyn, St Ives, Cornwall

- **Ian Hamilton Finlay**, Little Sparta, Dunsyre, Lanarkshire

Grow Raspberries

Pot-grown raspberry plants are available all year round but the most economical way of growing your own delicious berries is to start them from bare-root plants known as canes. On sale from late autumn until early spring, they will thrive in a sunny or partly shaded spot, and are ideal trained against walls and fences or planted in raised beds.

THREE GREAT RASPBERRY VARIETIES TO TRY

1 'All Gold' - a raspberry that tastes and looks good, thanks to its heavy crops of sweet golden fruit produced from mid-August until October.

2 'Glencoe' - forms a tight clump of spine-free canes with purple berries in summer.

3 'Polka' - renowned for its large yields of very big, aromatic berries between July and October.

SUMMER & AUTUMN RASPBERRIES

Raspberry varieties are split into two groups, based on when they fruit. Summer varieties produce berries from the end of June until August, while autumn raspberries bear fruit from August until mid-October. Apart from varieties with red fruit, there are also yellow, gold, orange, purple and black ones.

A POTTED HISTORY OF RASPBERRIES

A member of the Rosaceae plant family, raspberry plants can be found growing wild in Europe, Asia and North America. Most of the commercial varieties grown in the UK are cultivars of the European red raspberry (*Rubus idaeus*), which some historians believe was first brought to Britain by the Romans.

In the past, raspberries were not just considered good to eat but were believed to have medicinal properties. For example, in 1652, herbalist Nicholas Culpepper wrote: 'the fruit has a pleasant grateful smell and taste, is cordial and strengthens the stomach, stays vomiting and is good to prevent miscarriage'.

PLANTING CANES

Plant canes 45cm (18in) apart in shallow holes, about 30cm (12in) wide and 7.5cm (3in) deep – the old soil mark on the stems should be level with the surface of the soil. Spread out the roots, cover with soil, firm and water. To encourage fresh growth from beneath the ground, cut stems back to 23cm (9in) above soil level.

PROVIDING SUPPORT

Summer-fruiting raspberries are best trained against a post-and-wire support fence. Drive a 1.8m (6ft)-tall tree stake into the ground at either end of the row of raspberry canes and run two wires between the stakes at heights of 60cm (2ft) and 1.2m (4ft). Autumn raspberries don't grow as tall, so there's no need to shore them up.

GENERAL UPKEEP

Scatter some general-purpose fertilizer over the ground to boost growth in late winter and tie the stems of summer fruiters vertically to support wires, using garden twine. Keep the plants well-watered during dry spells, especially when fruit appears or the crop is likely to be disappointing.

PRUNING RASPBERRY CANES

Summer fruiters bear fruit on stems produced the previous year, so cut back spent stems to ground level once harvesting is over, leaving any green shoots to provide next year's crop.

Autumn-fruiting varieties produce fruit on the current year's growth, which emerges from the ground in spring. Keep plants healthy, within bounds and productive by chopping back the stems to ground level once the fruit has been picked.

GREAT GRAPE VINE

Hampton Court Palace has many attractions but plant lovers shouldn't miss the Great Vine, a magnificent BLACK HAMBURG (now called 'Schiava Grossa') grape vine that was planted for George III by 'Capability' Brown in 1768. Measuring 36.5m (120ft) long with a 4m (13ft)-circumference trunk, it is thought to be the largest vine in the world and can produce up to 1,000 bunches of grapes. This magnificent beast has been enjoyed by visitors since the 1840s from a viewing gallery set in the corner of a large glasshouse.

↓ Check bare-root raspberry canes are at the right level in the ground by laying a bamboo cane across the hole to see whether it is level with the old soil mark on the stems.

'What good is the warmth of summer,
without the cold of winter to give it sweetness?'

(John Steinbeck, *Travels with Charley: In Search of America*)

THE MONTH AT A GLANCE

- Plant hippeastrum bulbs indoors (see page 235).
- Water pot-grown Christmas trees regularly (see Look After Pot-grown Christmas Trees, pages 232).
- Take root cuttings from shrubs and perennials (see How to Take Root Cuttings, page 238).
- Prune tree branches (see How to Prune Tree Branches, page 240).
- Chop back lanky shrubs by one-half, to prevent windrock (see When to Prune Shrubs, page 29).
- Prune off shoots of camellia if leaves are marked with bright yellow patches, to prevent the spread of yellow mottle virus.
- Re-firm spring-flowering bedding plants that may have been lifted by frost.
- Loosen any ties that are digging into the bark of fruit trees.
- Sow seeds of winter salads (see Raise Some Winter Salads, page 245).
- Sweep up leaves from paths and lawns.
- Renew rusting wires used to train fruit against walls or fences.
- Keep off the lawn in frosty weather, to avoid damaging the grass.
- Water outdoor containers if the weather has been dry.
- Allow compost to completely dry out before watering poinsettias, to prevent colour loss and leaf drop (see Revive your Poinsettia for Next Year, page 233).
- Regularly top up bird feeders with nuts and seed mixes.
- Clean up dirty pots so they are ready to use in spring.
- Water greenhouse plants frugally, to avoid damp conditions that could lead to fungal diseases.
- Make sure greenhouse heaters are switched on, to prevent freezing temperatures damaging plants overnight (see Get Greenhouses Winter-ready, page 215).
- Check cold frames and cloches for slugs and snails.
- Place indoor plants close to a window to ensure they get as much light as possible.

December

So here it is...that time of year dominated by
preparations for the festive period ahead. As a
result, it's sometimes hard to find any spare time
to carry out any gardening, but don't worry –
there's really not that much to do outside and
nothing that can't wait until you've taken the
tinsel off the Christmas tree. This is the moment
to relax and enjoy being indoors, and gardening
should really be carried out only if you need some
fresh air or are looking for an excuse to escape a
family get-together for five minutes.

Look After Pot-grown Christmas trees

Container-grown Christmas trees are rising in popularity and are a good choice if you have room to display them outdoors once the festive season is over. Before parting with any cash, check that the tree is well-rooted. Give it a little tug to see if it's well anchored and look for roots poking out of the drainage holes at the bottom. Unfortunately, some Christmas trees are dug up and plunged into pots prior to going on sale - lifting from the field is usually carried out mechanically with trees losing most of their root system in the process. As a result, they are unlikely to live for very long.

In terms of looking after them, living trees hate central heating, so leave Christmas trees outdoors for as long as possible. Ideally, bring them inside a few days before the big day and don't keep them in the house any longer than 12 days. Treat them like a houseplant and water regularly. After Christmas, either plant the tree in the garden or move it into a slightly larger container.

A POTTED HISTORY OF CHRISTMAS TREES

Nobody really knows when the tradition of displaying trees indoors began, but records show that it was established in Germany as far back as the 15th century. The custom moved to Britain in 1800, when German-born Charlotte of Mecklenburg-Strelitz, wife of George III, decorated a cut tree for a festive gathering. Those moving in royal circles took on the custom, but it didn't catch on among the rest of the population until 1848, when a drawing of Queen Victoria and her family standing around an indoor tree appeared in the *Illustrated London News*. The tree was topped with an angel and decorated with candles, paper chains and sweets.

Revive Your Poinsettia for Next Year

Poinsettias are our most popular seasonal houseplant, with millions of them snapped up during the festive season. They are grown for their colourful bracts, which are modified leaves whose role in nature is to attract pollinating insects to the plant's tiny yellow flowerheads. Many people treat poinsettias as temporary residents and dump them once the bracts start to fade, usually in February or March. However, if you're prepared to give them some attention, it's possible to keep plants going so you end up with a bigger better specimen the following winter. To do this, continue to water the plant as necessary. In April, prune stems down to 10cm (4in) and transplant into a slightly larger pot filled with three parts peat-free potting compost to one part horticultural grit. Place the pot in a cool shady spot outdoors over summer. Bring back indoors in early September and position in a cool spot out of direct sunlight. Poinsettias need about 14 hours of darkness a night to produce their showy bracts, so place a box over the plant in the evening and remove it in the morning. Do this for eight weeks, then remove the box and display the plant in a warm room, out of direct sunlight and away from radiators.

A POTTED HISTORY OF POINSETTIAS

A native of Mexico, where they thrive in tropical forests, poinsettias are known botanically as *Euphorbia pulcherrima*. Its more familiar common name is a salute to Joel Roberts Poinsett, a 19th-century American diplomat and amateur botanist. He discovered the plant in 1828, following his appointment as the first US ambassador to Mexico. Long before this, poinsettias were important to the Aztec people. The bracts were crushed to make a red dye for fabrics and Montezuma II, ruler of the empire in the early 16th century, used poinsettia plants to decorate his palaces. They became popular in the USA in the early 20th century, thanks to nurseryman Albert Ecke, who treated them as a cut flower crop to sell at Christmas time. Poinsettias became a staple part of American festive celebrations in the 1960s, when his grandson Paul developed varieties suitable for growing in pots.

In Mexico, poinsettias are known colloquially as *flor de Nochebuena* (Christmas Eve plant). In one legend, a peasant girl was upset as she didn't have a gift to take to a midnight mass service. Apparently, an angel took pity on her and told her to pick some weeds. She did as she was told, took them to church and placed them on an altar. As she did so, the weeds transformed into the instantly recognizable green and red plants.

What Kind of Soil Do I Have?

Knowing what type of soil you have will have a big impact on what you can grow successfully. The three most common types of soil are clay, sandy and silty. A rough and ready way to find out what soil you have is to dig a bit up and try to roll it into a ball.

If the soil is sticky and can be moulded into a ball, then it's a loamy clay soil, while a heavy clay soil can be smoothed out quite thinly without falling apart. These soils are fairly fertile, but heavy clay can become waterlogged in winter and can dry rock-solid in summer.

If the soil feels gritty and doesn't hold together when you try and form it into a ball, then you have sandy soil. This tends to be well-drained, light and easy to cultivate but doesn't hold onto water and nutrients.

Silty soil feels silky when rubbed in the hands, and it sticks together. It's generally fertile and holds onto moisture, but compacts easily, causing drainage problems.

CHECK YOUR PH

The acidity of soil is recorded on a pH scale of 1-14. A pH of seven indicates that the soil is neutral with scale points above this being alkaline and anything beneath it signalling that the soil is acidic. Most plants prefer a pH of between 6.5 and 7.

An easy way to discover the pH of your soil is to carry out a simple test. There are various testing kits available, which vary in their sophistication. A cheap one will give you a rough indication, while an electronic gadget will provide a more accurate reading. If you have a large garden, it's worth carrying out tests in several places, as the pH can change within the same location.

The term 'garden makeover' entered the gardeners' lexicon in 1997 with the launch of Ground Force, a TV phenomenon presented by Alan Titchmarsh, Charlie Dimmock and Tommy Walsh. Attracting 12 million viewers at its peak, the show saw the trio turn up at someone's garden when they were away, give it an overhaul within two days and then surprise the owners on their return. It ran until 2005.

Plant Hippeastrum Bulbs

Originating from Central and South America, hippeastrums (commonly known as amaryllis) boast exotic flowers in a wide range of colours and shapes, from large trumpets to those with thin wispy petals. They are displayed on stout stalks that measure anywhere from 15cm (6in) to 1m (3ft) in height. Grown from bulbs that are readily available in late autumn and winter, these tender beauties are treated as houseplants in the UK. As their bulbs are huge, pick a container that's wide and deep enough for one to fit in comfortably. Set in peat-free potting compost combined with a handful of perlite, ensuring the head and shoulders of the bulb remain above the surface.

Water the compost and place the pot on a cool, south-facing windowsill. Over the next few weeks, a flower stalk will develop. When buds appear, feed every seven days with a weak solution of high-potash fertilizer. Allow the stalk to die back naturally before pulling it away from the bulb. The foliage will continue to grow, so keep watering and feeding weekly with a general-purpose fertilizer. In early autumn, the leaves will start to turn yellow. Allow the compost to completely dry out and let the foliage die back. When flower shoots appear in a few months' time, start the growing process again.

→ Make sure the head and shoulders of hippeastrum bulbs are above the surface of the compost.

Success with Hollies

Hollies (*Ilex*) are a symbol of the festive season and can be relied upon to brighten up winter with their evergreen foliage and jewel-like berries. Common holly (*I. aquifolium*) is the species everyone knows with its spiky, dark green leaves and scarlet fruit, but there are actually hundreds of different hollies and these vary enormously in their looks. Leaves can be prickly at the edges, smooth or completely covered in spines, and they can measure anywhere from the width of a fingernail up to the length of a hand. Some have white-, silver- or yellow-variegated leaves. Apart from red berries, there are also yellow, white, orange and even black-fruited varieties.

All hollies prefer moist, well-drained, sandy soil, but will grow in virtually anything apart from very wet ground. As they hate being moved, plant them in the right spot to avoid the need for transplanting; golden variegated hollies like full sun, while silver varieties are best in semi-shade. All-green ones can cope with sun or dappled shade. Due to their vigour, most hollies are unsuitable as long-term subjects for pots. The exception is Japanese holly (*I. crenata*), a slow-growing member of the genus.

DID YOU KNOW ?

Fans of Downton Abbey might not know that the location for the historical drama was the birthplace of an important race of hollies. In 1838, a hybrid of common holly (*Ilex aquifolium*) and *I. perado* subsp. perado (a species from the Canary Islands) was identified at Highclere Castle in Berkshire and named *I. × altaclerensis* (the name derives from *Alta Clera*, medieval Latin for Highclere). Highclere hollies are admired for their rounded, spine-free leaves, and varieties include *I. × a.* 'W J Bean' and *I. × a.* 'Balearica'.

HOLLY LEGENDS

Our native holly is steeped in folklore. In Celtic mythology, the holly king ruled from the summer to winter solstice, when the oak king defeated him to reign for the next six months. In traditional Christmas Mummers' plays, the holly king is portrayed as a giant covered in holly leaves and wielding a holly tree as a club. The custom for displaying holly branches indoors was first carried out by the Romans during their festival of Saturnalia in December, and was later adopted by early Christians, who saw great symbolism in the plant – the prickly leaves were said to represent the crown of thorns worn by Jesus and the berries his spilt blood.

LET'S TALK ABOUT SEX

Before buying a holly, check to find out the plant's gender. Female plants produce berries, while male plants do not and are grown solely for their foliage. However, to ensure a female holly bears fruit, you need a male plant nearby to assist fertilization. To help pick the right plants, the *RHS Plant Finder* helpfully puts an (m) or (f) next to entries. If you have space for only one tree and want berries, opt for *Ilex aquifolium* 'J C van Tol', *I. aquifolium* 'Pyramidalis' and *I.* 'Nellie R Stevens' - all are self-fertile.

FIVE HANDSOME HOLLIES TO TRY

1 *I. × altaclerensis* **'Golden King' (f)** - almost spineless, gold-edged leaves.

2 *I. aquifolium* **'Bacciflava' (f)** - near spineless leaves and yellow fruit.

3 *I. aquifolium* **'Ferox Argentea' (m)** - spiny, cream-edged leaves that are barbed on the surface.

4 *I. aquifolium* **'Golden Queen' (m)** - spiny-edged leaves that are edged with gold.

5 *I. aquifolium* **'Silver Milkmaid' (f)** - large red berries and small, spiny, curved leaves that have white splashes.

Name explain:
John Innes

John Innes is not a brand of compost but a type of soil-based compost named in honour of John Innes, a property developer with a passion for gardening. Upon his death in 1904, his home in Merton Park, Surrey, was bequeathed to the Board of Agriculture and turned into the John Innes Horticultural Institution. It was here, in the mid-1930s, that scientists William Lawrence and John Newell invented John Innes compost, and the recipe played a big part in the government's Dig for Victory campaign during the Second World War. The institution is now called the John Innes Centre and is based in Norwich.

How to Take Root Cuttings

Winter is the perfect time to propagate a wide range of flowering perennials by taking root cuttings, a technique that involves removing lengths of root from underground, snipping them to size and then inserting them into pots, where they will form new roots and shoots.

To propagate perennials with thick roots, lift a clump of them and sever a few long roots close to the crown. Divide into 5cm (2in) pieces, making a flat cut where the root was severed from its parent and a sloping one at the other end. Insert five cuttings into a 7.5cm (3in) pot filled with potting compost, making sure the flat end is facing upward and is level with the surface. Cover with a thin layer of horticultural grit.

Plants with finer roots need a different treatment. As they're too flexible to be pushed upright into compost, position 5-7.5cm (2-3in)-long pieces horizontally on the surface of 12cm (5in) pots filled with compost. Set the cuttings 4cm (1½in) apart so they have plenty of space - shoots will develop along the whole length of the cutting.

Place pots in a cold frame, unheated greenhouse or front porch. Shoots will appear within a few weeks, but wait until roots start poking their way out of the drainage holes in the base before splitting up the rootball and moving each cutting to its own pot. Plants should be ready for planting out by summer.

TEN PERENNIALS TO PROPAGATE BY ROOT CUTTINGS

1 bear's breeches (*Acanthus*)

2 bloody cranesbill (*Geranium sanguineum*)

3 brunnera

4 drumstick primula (*Primula denticulata*)

5 Japanese anemone (*Anemone × hybrida*)

6 mullein (*Verbascum*)

7 Oriental poppies (*Papaver orientale*)

8 phlox

9 sea holly (*Eryngium*)

10 tree poppy (*Romneya*)

↓ To make sure root cuttings are not planted upside down, divide long roots into smaller pieces with a flat cut at the top and a slanted cut below.

How to Prune Tree Branches

If you need to restore the symmetry of a tree by removing a branch, use the three-cut method to do this smoothly. Saw halfway through from underneath the branch, 45cm (18in) from the trunk. Then saw all the way through from the top, 2.5cm (1in) further along from the undercut, toward the tree trunk. End by cutting back the stub close, but not flush, to the trunk.

Attempting to cut through large branches in one go from above is likely to cause bark to tear underneath, potentially damaging the trunk.

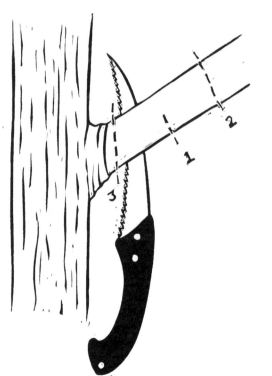

←

1 Saw halfway through the branch from underneath.

2 Completely cut through the branch from above.

3 Saw through the branch, cutting close to the trunk.

Pest and Disease Watch: Mealy Bug

Probably the most common pest
affecting houseplants, mealy bugs are
sap-sucking insects that secrete a white
waxy substance which makes them
appear like little patches of cotton wool.
If you spot the bugs early enough, you
should be able to rub them off by hand.
Treat plants with an organic pesticide
if they are infested, making sure you
spray under leaves, leaf joints and other
relatively inaccessible places.

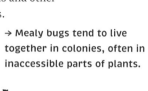

→ Mealy bugs tend to live
together in colonies, often in
inaccessible parts of plants.

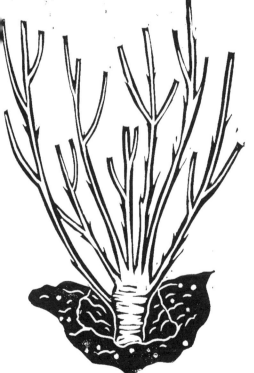

↑ Draw soil back into the gap
and firm back into place.

Deal with Windrock

Newly planted trees, shrubs and
perennials are vulnerable to so-called
windrock, where relentless buffeting
backward and forward leads to a gap
opening up around the stem and the
soil. The movement itself can harm
roots and relax the plant's grip in the
ground, and the cavity acts as an entry
point for frost. Check susceptible plants
regularly and re-firm them in the ground
if they have been loosened. Overly lanky,
established buddleias, roses (*Rosa*),
hydrangeas and mallows (*Lavatera*) are
also prone to windrock. Prevent damage
by pruning stems back by about one-
third, to lighten their load - these plants
can then be pruned properly in spring.

Eat Your Sprouts

Brussels sprouts divide people like few other vegetables. Some can't get enough of the tight green buttons, while others can't stand the things and will just about tolerate the sight of them at Christmas dinner. Nobody knows for sure where this member of the brassica family – along with cabbages, kale and cauliflowers – originates from, although some botanists think they are a natural mutation of cabbages that arose in Belgium during the 16th century.

What isn't in any doubt is that sprouts are something of a superfood. The little green balls are a great source of vitamins A and K and, gram for gram, contain nearly 50 per cent more vitamin C than oranges. They are low in calories, high in fibre and packed full of antioxidants and minerals. To grow your own, start seed indoors between February and May, or snap up young plants in spring.

→ Sprouts can take up to eight months to reach maturity.

Disease-resistant Vegetables

There's been a lot of breeding work over the past few years to create vegetables that are tolerant, or even resistant, to pests and diseases. These varieties are a godsend to gardeners who have had a problem growing certain veggies in the past or who are new to growing their own food and want a greater degree of certainty that whatever they plant is going to succeed. Whichever camp you're in, it's a good idea to consider these scientific developments when putting orders together for what to grow in spring.

Tomatoes are one of the most popular crops for any vegetable gardener to grow, but they are at the mercy of blight. 'Ferline', 'Mountain Magic' and 'Crimson Crush' have great tolerance to this disease, which can destroy foliage and fruit. Blight is also a problem with potatoes in warm wet summers, but there are several varieties that are worth trying if you've ever lost crops to this disease. 'Sarpo Mira', 'Setanta' and 'Cara' all grow so vigorously that they are able to cope with blight much better, and an attack is unlikely to wipe out your crop.

Courgette 'Tosca' has good tolerance to powdery mildew (see page 67), carrot 'Flyaway' is resistant to carrot fly and 'Kilaton' is a club-root resistant cabbage. 'Passandra' is an indomitable cucumber with resistance to powdery mildew, downy mildew and mosaic virus.

Word buster:
Cultivar

This is a plant variety that has arisen through breeding and is a portmanteau of 'cultivated variety'. Cultivar names are generally enclosed within single quotation marks as in *Acer palmatum* 'Bloodgood'.

Colourful Crab Apples

Few trees brighten up the winter garden like crab apples (*Malus*). When stripped of foliage, their bare branches reveal masses of glossy colourful fruit, which often lasts well into the new year. These fruits come in many shapes, colours and sizes. There are varieties with red, yellow, orange, purple or two-tone skin, with fruit measuring 1-5cm (½-2in) across. Many look like miniature apples, while others are conical or even pear-shaped. Crab apples are native to Europe, Asia and North America, and one species is also indigenous to Britain - European crab apple (*M. sylvestris*) - which can sometimes be spotted in ancient hedgerows, scrubland or growing in the open.

Like many wild plants, crab apple trees are steeped in folklore. The Druids considered them sacred and made wands from their wood, and branches were burned by Celts during fertility rites. Some country folk believed that finding a crab apple tree in flower during autumn was a harbinger of death. During the late 1200s, the Lord of Egremont began a tradition of giving away free crab apples to the poor of the parish. The Egremont Crab Fair in Cumbria is now one of the oldest fairs in the country.

FIVE CRACKING CRAB APPLES TO TRY

1 **'Butterball'** - bred in the USA and in cultivation since 1961, this variety produces pink-flushed, white flowers in spring and has large yellow fruit that remains on the branches long after the leaves have fallen.

2 **'Evereste'** - introduced in the early 1980s, the branches are laden with 2.5cm (1in)-wide, red-flushed, orange-yellow fruit, which persists well into winter and is great for making crab-apple jelly.

3 **'Laura'** - developed in Kent, this naturally compact variety has purplish foliage and two-tone, pink and white flowers in spring, followed by maroon fruit in autumn.

4 **Red Obelisk** - a compact tree with a distinct upright habit and branches laden with light pink flowers, which turn into conical red fruit. The foliage starts off bronze before maturing to dark green.

5 *M. × zumi* **'Golden Hornet'** - making its debut in 1949, this variety has pink-flushed, white blossom in spring followed by bright yellow fruit about the size of a little fingernail.

Raise Some Winter Salads

Summer salads will curl up their toes at the mere mention of frost, but there are some leafy greens that are much more tolerant of colder conditions. Among these leafy crops are lamb's lettuce, mustards, robust forms of lettuce, purple mizuna, tatsoi and komatsuna.

One of the hardiest of the lot is winter purslane, an edible annual that tolerates temperatures as low as -15°C (5°F). Its heart-shaped leaves are juicy, with a mild sweet flavour. Seeds can be sown in the ground or pots. Don't worry if they're a little sluggish to get going – winter salads don't grow as fast or as vigorously as those sown in summer, and the weather can hold them back. Keep the soil or compost moist but avoid overwatering, to prevent rotting. If frost is forecast, cover crops in the ground with low polythene tunnels or horticultural fleece, while pots should be moved into a greenhouse or front porch, or even stood on a kitchen windowsill.

December Gems

Add some seasonal interest to your garden with this selection of plants named after the first month of winter.

- daffodil (*Narcissus*) 'December Bride' – has white tepals and a pink corona.

- elder (*Sambucus*) '14th December' – produces purplish leaves and pretty pink flowers.

- heather (*Erica carnea*) 'December Red' – has blue-green foliage and pink flowers.

- *Viburnum farreri* 'December Dwarf' – bears sweetly scented, pinky white flowers.

- white spruce (*Picea glauca*) 'December' – a dwarf conical tree with dark green needles.

'Do not spread the compost on the weeds.'

William Shakespeare, *Hamlet*

Crop Planner

VEGETABLES

ASPARAGUS (SEE PAGE 54)

	J	F	M	A	M	J	J	A	S	O	N	D
Plant crowns			x	x								
Harvest				x	x	x						

BEETROOT (SEE PAGE 130)

	J	F	M	A	M	J	J	A	S	O	N	D
Sow				x	x	x	x					
Harvest						x	x	x	x			

BROAD BEANS (SEE PAGE 202)

	J	F	M	A	M	J	J	A	S	O	N	D
Sow			x	x						x	x	
Harvest					x	x	x					

BRUSSELS SPROUTS (SEE PAGE 202)

	J	F	M	A	M	J	J	A	S	O	N	D
Sow		x	x	x								
Plant					x	x						
Harvest	x	x	x						x	x	x	x

CABBAGES, SPRING (SEE PAGE 181)

	J	F	M	A	M	J	J	A	S	O	N	D
Sow							x	x				
Plant									x	x		
Harvest			x	x	x							

CARROTS (SEE PAGE 86)

	J	F	M	A	M	J	J	A	S	O	N	D
Sow				x	x	x	x	x				
Harvest					x	x	x	x	x	x	x	

COURGETTES (SEE PAGE 124)

	J	F	M	A	M	J	J	A	S	O	N	D
Sow				(i)	(i)							
Plant				x	x							
Harvest						x	x	x	x			

FRENCH BEANS (SEE PAGE 104)

	J	F	M	A	M	J	J	A	S	O	N	D
Sow				x	x	x	x					
Harvest					x	x	x	x				

GARLIC (SEE PAGE 204)

	J	F	M	A	M	J	J	A	S	O	N	D
Plant	x	x	x							x	x	x
Harvest					x	x	x	x				

ONIONS (SEE PAGE 66)

	J	F	M	A	M	J	J	A	S	O	N	D
Plant sets			x	x								
Harvest							x	x				

PEAS (SEE PAGE 89)

	J	F	M	A	M	J	J	A	S	O	N	D
Sow			(u)	x	x	x	x					
Harvest						x	x	x				

(i) = Sow indoors.
(u) = Sow undercover, outdoors. Protect with a cloche or low polythene tunnel.

POTATOES, FIRST EARLY (SEE PAGE 34)

	J	F	M	A	M	J	J	A	S	O	N	D
Plant tubers			x	x								
Harvest				x	x	x						

POTATOES, SECOND EARLY (SEE PAGE 34)

	J	F	M	A	M	J	J	A	S	O	N	D
Plant tubers				x								
Harvest						x	x	x	x			

POTATOES, MAINCROP (SEE PAGE 34)

	J	F	M	A	M	J	J	A	S	O	N	D
Plant tubers			x									
Harvest									x	x	x	

PUMPKINS & WINTER SQUASHES (SEE PAGE 106)

	J	F	M	A	M	J	J	A	S	O	N	D
Sow				(i)								
Plant					x	x						
Harvest										x		

RHUBARB (SEE PAGE 82)

	J	F	M	A	M	J	J	A	S	O	N	D
Plant	x	x	x							x	x	x
Harvest			x	x	x							
Harvest (forced rhubarb)		x										

RUNNER BEANS (SEE PAGE 126)

	J	F	M	A	M	J	J	A	S	O	N	D
Sow				(i)	x							
Plant				x	x							
Harvest						x	x	x	x			

SHALLOTS (SEE PAGE 32)

	J	F	M	A	M	J	J	A	S	O	N	D
Plant sets		x	x									
Harvest						x	x					

SWEETCORN (SEE PAGE 108)

	J	F	M	A	M	J	J	A	S	O	N	D
Sow					X (mid-May)	X (early June)						
Harvest							x	x	x			

SWISS CHARD (SEE PAGE 164)

	J	F	M	A	M	J	J	A	S	O	N	D
Sow			x	x	x	x	x					
Harvest	x	x	x			x	x	x	x	x	x	

SALAD VEGETABLES

CUCUMBERS, INDOORS (SEE PAGE 64)

	J	F	M	A	M	J	J	A	S	O	N	D
Sow		(i)	(i)	(i)								
Plant					x							
Harvest						x	x	x	x			

CUCUMBERS, OUTDOORS (SEE PAGE 64)

	J	F	M	A	M	J	J	A	S	O	N	D
Sow				(i)								
Plant					x	x						
Harvest						x	x	x				

PEPPERS, CHILLI AND SWEET (SEE PAGE 58)

	J	F	M	A	M	J	J	A	S	O	N	D
Sow		(i)	(i)										
Plant					x	x						
Harvest					x	x	x	x				

RADISHES (SEE PAGE 122)

	J	F	M	A	M	J	J	A	S	O	N	D
Sow			x	x	x	x	x	x	x			
Harvest					x	x	x	x	x	x		

ROCKET (SEE PAGE 158)

	J	F	M	A	M	J	J	A	S	O	N	D
Sow			x	x	x	x	x	x	x			
Harvest				x	x	x	x	x	x	x	x	

SALAD LEAVES, MIXED (SEE PAGE 121)

	J	F	M	A	M	J	J	A	S	O	N	D
Sow			(u)	x	x	x	x	x	(u)			
Harvest					x	x	x	x	x	x		

SALAD LEAVES, WINTER (SEE PAGE 121)

	J	F	M	A	M	J	J	A	S	O	N	D
Sow								(u)	(u)	(u)		
Harvest	x	x	x								x	x

SPRING ONIONS (SEE PAGE 157)

	J	F	M	A	M	J	J	A	S	O	N	D
Sow			x	x	x	x	x	x				
Harvest						x	x	x	x			

TOMATOES (SEE PAGE 60)

	J	F	M	A	M	J	J	A	S	O	N	D
Sow			(i)	(i)								
Plant					x	x						
Harvest							x	x	x	x		

HERBS

BASIL (SEE PAGE 52)

	J	F	M	A	M	J	J	A	S	O	N	D
Sow		(i)	(i)	(i)	(i)	(i)						
Plant				x	x	x	x					
Harvest						x	x	x	x	x		

CHIVES (SEE PAGE 88)

	J	F	M	A	M	J	J	A	S	O	N	D
Sow			(i)	(i)	(i)							
Plant				x	x	x						
Harvest				x	x	x	x	x	x			

MINT (SEE PAGE 121)

	J	F	M	A	M	J	J	A	S	O	N	D
Plant				x	x					x	x	
Harvest				x	x	x	x	x	x			

PARSLEY, IN POTS (SEE PAGE 154)

	J	F	M	A	M	J	J	A	S	O	N	D
Sow			x	x	x	x	x	x				
Harvest	(u)	(u)	X	X	x	x	x	x	x	x	(u)	(u)

ROSEMARY (SEE PAGE 120)

	J	F	M	A	M	J	J	A	S	O	N	D
Plant				x	x	x	x					
Harvest	x	x	x	x	x	x	x	x	x	x	x	x

THYME (SEE PAGE 139)

	J	F	M	A	M	J	J	A	S	O	N	D
Plant				x	x	x	x					
Harvest	x	x	x	x	x	x	x	x	x	x	x	x

FRUIT

APPLES (SEE PAGE 50)

	J	F	M	A	M	J	J	A	S	O	N	D
Plant	x	x	x							x	x	x
Harvest								x	x	x	x	

BLACKBERRIES (SEE PAGE 206)

	J	F	M	A	M	J	J	A	S	O	N	D
Plant	x	x	x							x	x	x
Harvest							x	x	x			

BLUEBERRIES (SEE PAGE 207)

	J	F	M	A	M	J	J	A	S	O	N	D
Plant	x	x	x							x	x	x
Harvest						x	x	x				

FIGS (SEE PAGE 36)

	J	F	M	A	M	J	J	A	S	O	N	D
Plant			x	x	x					x	x	
Harvest								x	x			

PEARS (SEE PAGE 50)

	J	F	M	A	M	J	J	A	S	O	N	D
Plant	x	x	x							x	x	x
Harvest								x	x	x	x	

RASPBERRIES (SEE PAGE 227)

	J	F	M	A	M	J	J	A	S	O	N	D
Plant	x	x	x							x	x	x
Harvest						x	x	x	x			

STRAWBERRIES (SEE PAGE 80)

	J	F	M	A	M	J	J	A	S	O	N	D
Plant			x	x	x		x	x	x	x		
Harvest					x	x	x	x	x			

Index

Acknowledgements

As the captain of a men's tennis team, I'm all too fond of using the phrase 'there's no I in team'. Well, making a book is certainly a team effort, and I would like to thank my awesome editor Sarah Kyle and designer Yasia Williams, along with Heather Tempest-Elliott, who has brought my words to life with her beautiful illustrations. A big, big debt of gratitude must go to Alison Starling, who responded positively to my initial idea and helped to develop it into the book that's now in your hands.

Writing a book is a time-consuming process and it sometimes involves keeping unsociable hours or not being available to do family things at weekends. Therefore, a big thanks must go to my long-suffering partner, Alis. A special mention must go to our two children, Louis and Lily, who after being bribed, would buy me more writing time by walking our two dogs, Ollie and Lisla.

Lastly, but certainly not least, a huge thank you to my parents Paul and Joy, for sparking a love of gardening in me as a child that still burns strongly today.